PILGRIMAGE TO INDIA

PILGRIMAGE TO INDIA

Lessons Learned and Now Lived

Rev. John J. Lombardi

Copyright © 2020 by Rev. John J. Lombardi.

ISBN:	Hardcover	978-1-6641-3878-0
	Softcover	978-1-6641-3879-7
	eBook	978-1-6641-3877-3

All rights reserved. No part of this book may be reproduced or transmitted in any form or by any means, electronic or mechanical, including photocopying, recording, or by any information storage and retrieval system, without permission in writing from the copyright owner.

Any people depicted in stock imagery provided by Getty Images are models, and such images are being used for illustrative purposes only.
Certain stock imagery © Getty Images.

New American Bible, revised edition © 2010, 1991, 1986, 1970 Confraternity of Christian Doctrine, Washington, D.C. and are used by permission of the copyright owner. All Rights Reserved. No part of the New American Bible may be reproduced in any form without permission in writing from the copyright owner.

Print information available on the last page.

Rev. date: 11/17/2020

To order additional copies of this book, contact:
Xlibris
844-714-8691
www.Xlibris.com
Orders@Xlibris.com

CONTENTS

Acknowledgements vii
Introduction… Or, Life is Like That! xi

Chapter 1   Initial Inspirations 1
Chapter 2   Spirituality, Theology and God 13
Chapter 3   It's All Part of The Pilgrimage 63
Chapter 4   Giving is Receiving 74
Chapter 5   Roll with The Punches 84
Chapter 6   Adventure 96
Chapter 7   Teamwork 103
Chapter 8   Detachment 107
Chapter 9   Universality 114
Chapter 10 Conclusions 124

ACKNOWLEDGEMENTS

To my editor, Margie Redmond, who went far beyond the call of duty: Blessings upon you! Thank you for your considerable skills that made this book possible.

For my fellow pilgrims who went with me to India on various trips, you inspired and helped me: Paul, Kevin, Pam, and so many others. May God bless you!

<u>Bible translations</u> from: New American Bible USCCB, online

Martin Luther King, once noted he was a
tourist in most of his journeys,
but said he went to India as a *pilgrim*.

INTRODUCTION...
OR, LIFE IS LIKE THAT!

This Book is about insights gained from my three trips to India – my very first pilgrimage in 1993, when I traversed the entire subcontinent; my second trip there in 2005; and my trip covered most especially in this book, during a two-week pilgrimage in January, 2009.

After returning to the United States from my last pilgrimage, I thought about those many India-esque experiences – such as trying to pray while buzzing through Calcutta streets, working on my patience during the inevitable flight delays, or my sometimes-unsuccessful bargaining with frenzied street vendors.

There were so many Indian-incidents which affected me. The goal: How do I capture them to the benefit of others *and* apply those lessons learned toward discussing life in general today? It's a tall order, but not impossible; after all, many of these experiences reminded me of people back home or elsewhere – they're not just incidents confined to my own life.

India is stimulating on many levels: Spiritually, physically, culturally, and I was thinking, Dear Reader, that you might find some of these stories and events helpful, and no matter how unique or strange you might find these anecdotes, understand this, India really is that incredibly unique.

Here's a quick synopsis of my 2009 Pilgrimage, covered in detail in this book:

Funniest time. Ten of us pilgrims stuffed ourselves into a tiny taxi (slightly larger than a Volkswagen Beetle), and it careened through Calcutta streets for half-an-hour. We laughed the entire time—better than focusing on being so cramped! Painful, but fun—just like life.

Strangest time. The purgatory endured while waiting for our plane back to America, which never came, by the way, because of too much fog and pollution in Calcutta. Lesson learned? *Life is filled with curveballs. What is your reaction to tense situations?*

Most Dramatic. Celebrating morning Mass at the Motherhouse of Mother Teresa in Calcutta with a hundred nuns, pilgrims and western beatniks. Lesson? *Spiritual life is a fun adventure best shared with others.*

Peak moment. Seeing Kanchenjunga, the world's third-largest mountain, majestically resplendent, towering, even though we were a hundred miles away in Darjeeling. *Yes, all the travails are worth the trip.*

Most poignant moment. Praying at night at Mother Teresa's tomb, with various pilgrims solemnly kneeling, reflecting on her message. Lesson: *Life is somber-seriousness too.*

Most embarrassing moment. When two of us pilgrim-swimmers were kicked out of the pool at the very-ritzy Oberoi Hotel. While supremely privileged to travel, there was still an opportunity to be *persona non grata*!

Ironically, going so far away to India brought me closer to home, and to my true, deeper self – both the good and bad. I discovered yet again how irritable *and* how social I can be, and most especially, how much I love travelling and can still appreciate my world back home. Sometimes you *do* have to go far away to find yourself and blessings.

There are many things one can learn on pilgrimage, rather than on a vacation.

What's the difference? Well, pilgrimage demands that one must have a specific spiritual goal in mind. Vacation is usually non-specific and relaxation-oriented versus goal-fixated.

One of our college-aged pilgrims said, "It's strange you have to go so far way to learn something so simple – like about God's grace, the call to service, or practicing the presence of God… but it is precisely the contrast experience that happens during a pilgrimage, especially while learning about a different culture." Kevin, that pilgrim, was right. The "contrast experience" revealed layers of the false- or partial-self in ways that the repetitiously-familiar will not.

Case in point: we saw and enjoyed different manifestations of God through excellent-though-spicy Indian foods, the smells and bells of careening Calcutta city life and children playing happily in trash heaps.

One is challenged to be more daringly-open to different people and encountering wildly different experiences – like taking a tour of the brooding Kali Temple with Hindus and Brahmins watching me, a Roman Catholic priest, very closely.

This pilgrimage, in 2009, for me was one of dedication to God and service to others, and helped me discover deeper parts of myself. When I helped others, I saw and felt their needs and deprivations, very revealing lessons I would not have learned had I not made that journey to India.

LIFE IN MINIATURE

Maryland is sometimes called "America in miniature" – because it has a little bit of everything, as in mountains, an ocean-coast; small towns, big cities and rolling countryside. It has a diverse population of races and cultures – not to mention all four seasons.

With that in mind, it occurred to me that our pilgrimage was likewise for me a snapshot-portrait of life in miniature, and hopefully to you as well, Dear Reader. During our pilgrimage, it was filled with ecstatic events *and* epiphanic episodes; we met many different people and encountered familiar types, too. That's life.

Back in 2009, at first, I was a little reluctant to consider returning to India after my other two trips. I liked my daily comforts – the familiar groove of living in the modern West and in particular, being able to count on unpolluted water from the tap, and flush toilets and clean bathrooms – two things that don't always exist in India. I remembered the difficulties from before, however, India was still so tantalizingly attractive to me. Why think about going there again?

In any case, as I *did* go, here are elements of that pilgrimage – which occurred before, during and after our trip. They might illustrate my theme: *Life is Like That*.

- **Preparation for the journey.** Even before we left, we had the "*life is like that*" syndrome. Amongst us pilgrims, we held meetings, social gatherings and exchanged emails, and kept repeating our mantra: *This is a pilgrimage, not a vacation*. Our travel coordinator often ribbed us for not reading her emails, most of them marked "*Please read carefully and respond!*" When under such a penalty, one will perform, but not until the threat looms!
- **Working as a team.** Obviously, while preparing for India, there are many things we could not prepare for or foresee – flexibility is required. I slogged through notes of past trips for days, making lists, and consulting fellow travelers. In retrospect, I believe we did a fair job getting ahead of various speed-bumps, planning as a team, and so our "group-think" worked in our favor.
- **Being a helper.** It was good to meet other pilgrims just before going; after all, few knew of the other travelers. We tried to develop a spiritual and social synergy along the Way. This is a necessary process, whether a soccer team or musical group. In other words, no pilgrim was toact independently. We were to always travel in a group, with cell phones, with an emergency phone number if the need should arise to call it. However, since a group leader can't always anticipate several events happening simultaneously, human forgetfulness or carelessness, this didn't always happen! Case in point: I pulled a muscle in my calf while racing two other pilgrims (I was barefoot, no less, and didn't stretch beforehand, duh). Paul (who defeated me in the race) helped me with therapy and two other pilgrims found Indian healing muscle-relaxant cream from a local pharmacy. Fellow pilgrims help each other whenever or however possible. I wasn't

left behind. This is a life-lesson. All of us need to help others, even if that person isn't necessarily part of "your team". We each are called to build up and repair the Body of Christ.

- *Communication.* Whether going out for dinner with various group members, zig-zagging frantically through Indian train stations, dealing with someone getting sick and remaining behind, or suddenly changing our itinerary, we always had to communicate what was going on with everyone in the group. This was a constant process, to include re-communicating directions – dependent, of course, upon divergent developments or changing schedules.
- *Similar Mission.* We all had a focus – we were on a *pilgrimage*, not a vacation or religious tour. One way to remind us: We sought to *practice the presence of God*, especially through what we called "The Three S's": **S**ervice, **S**ocialization and **S**pirituality.

Service. We imitated the example of Mother Teresa's sisters, and served the poorest of the poor.

Socialization. While out and about, such as wandering the streets of Calcutta, playing pickup soccer, or visiting markets and interacting with the local culture, we spent time genuinely having fun with the people and enjoying activities with them.

Spirituality. Daily, we celebrated Mass in the morning and had evening prayers together. We also made holy hours and prayed the Rosary… and if that wasn't enough, we even planned a retreat-day for refreshment and renewal.

> **Food for thought**
>
> Do you have the "Three S's" in your life? Do you have *social*-interaction with others? Do you *serve* those who cannot repay you? Do you have a life of *spirituality* that includes regular, fervent prayer?

- ***Were we 'hooked' on India?*** Anywhere in the world, it's easy to get hooked on things—like television, the internet, gaming, drugs, social causes, sex, the news, hobbies, people—take your pick. It's not necessarily bad to get hooked on some things – it depends on *what* it is. The real trick: 'get hooked' on the right things for the right reasons – such as reading the Bible, developing holy habits, celebrating Mass and the sacraments, it's a good way to have a life of light and holiness.

The following chapters include "Initial Inspirations" followed by seven subjects which describe and discuss my time in India. Clearly, the longest and most intense-detailed is Chapter II, on Spirituality and God, which, obviously, any book on India must delve into. I will relate these reflections to what any person will experience in life. Remember the mantra which guides and hopefully inspires us:*Life is like that!*

Chapter 1: *Initial Inspirations.* What ignited me to go to India. There are many factors and, basically just a couple, so tune in below and find out.

Chapter 2:*Spirituality / God*. Life is about God, seeking and honoring Him and then bringing Him to others. Our pilgrimage was just so—a travelogue illustrating a *"documentation of Divinity"* – that is, encountering the Lord through prayer and fellowship in India.

Chapter 3: *Integration.* One of our mottos while traveling was: *It's all part of the Pilgrimage.* Whether confronting a trial, enjoying strange tea or Indian dal-and-rice, we tried to remember not to repel tough experiences but to integrate them into our pilgrimage and lives. We may not always understand *how* God is working in our lives at the time, but we may accept that He *is* working through mysterious ways.

Chapter4: *Giving/* **Service.** Part of life is about serving God and others. This is a way to become selfless. God gave us all kinds of opportunities to give ourselves away – and we certainly learned this on pilgrimage in stark and strange ways. We all can learn this in life, as we encounter God in others by the act of service.

Chapter 5: *Flexibility.* A familiar way to say this: "roll with the punches". One needs to be adaptable. This was certainly evident on our pilgrimage, dealing with many surprises, frustrations and epiphanies dealt to us by life in India. Expect the unexpected. This is the same in life.

Chapter 6: *Adventure.* Who wants to be bored? If where you are isn't very challenging, and seeking adventure is in your blood, then go to India! See new and wonderful things, cultivate zest on your quest.

Chapter 7: *Teamwork.* Christians can do more together, versus one person acting alone. When travelling, by necessity, one will eventually need help from fellow pilgrims. It's a way to learn how to rely on – and trust – others. This is especially true in a country where you don't know the language or local laws. Just like life.

Chapter 8: *Detachment.* Defined one way, this means letting go, or becoming un-attached. When you travel overseas, remember that things won't be like home. For some, this learning curve is steep, one must let go of those familiar "small ways" and learn new ones.

Chapter 9: *Universality.* Variety is the spice of life. In India, we met all kinds of people from all over the world, as we worked with the Missionary of Charity sisters. Pilgrims have unique stories to reveal – basically, a salad bowl of experiences that will surprise you.

Chapter 10: *Conclusions.* Basically, it's a discussion of what I took from my time in India, and how I changed, or could pt should change, and how to pass on the glorious lessons God gave me.

CHAPTER 1

*"Sometimes we forget we're on an adventure with
the Lord and that his presence is with us."
-Linda Evans Shepherd*

Initial Inspirations

So, you may ask, Just how did I get to India, and form my own kind of "Indian allure"? Well, initially, I studied philosophy in college, from 1978-1983 at Towson State University (north of Baltimore) —and dabbled in Eastern-mysticism, eventually becoming a major in philosophy and mass communication. Sometimes, I wondered where and when these pungent primeval truths originated. I had imagined what the source of the Hindu Vedas (some of the oldest holy writings of India) might be, how and where the Buddha actually lived. I had dreamed about the fabled saris and saffron-robed monks of India, and speculated within my mind about the Taj Mahal, Islam, Gandhi's peace movements and burning ghats on the Ganges River. I longed to visit the Himalayas and the deserts of central India. I wanted to go there.

Ten years after college, I did, in 1993. The plan? Travel all over the subcontinent. I started at Bengal-Calcutta, went on to Delhi (in the northern middle of the country) to Kashmir (the northern tier) to Bombay (west coast); to Kerala state (southwest coast) to Madras (southeast coast) to Varanasi and back to Calcutta. Originally, all this travel was to take place via train, however, I found this to be impractical, and extremely slow. The trains were way too overcrowded, always late, and undependable, plus the fact that India is a *giant* country. No way could I cover the entire country in a reasonable length of time, and within my budget. Then I stumbled upon an India Air-pass package that was good for twenty-one days. Perfect. I got to see most of the country after all – far beyond my original planning!

Speaking of planning, back in 1993, I remember getting sidetracked – a better word might be *hijacked* – while enroute to Bod Gaya, location of the Buddha's enlightenment. Being somewhat gullible, I relied on directions of some suspicious persons who told me to take a certain taxi-truck out of town and so forth. I went, and ended up about two hours off-course. I was extremely ticked off, but eventually became, well, mostly-enlightened—kinda', after calming and cooly recognizing, this is India, and then eventually reaching Bod Gaya.

Once I arrived, I met a young, beautiful Buddhist monk who showed me around, and in broken English, told me about the city, the Buddha, and his own personal vows and lifestyle. I recall walking across a dry river bed at sundown with him, quite the apex of my pilgrimage, in the Buddha's town getting a personal tour with a monk. Simple, serene and absolutely beautiful.

HOW THE "PERFECT STORM" CAME ABOUT...

My dreams were manifesting more acutely, and my studies in philosophy percolated anew within me, and I had been a priest for five years. It was now possible for me to arrange a mini-sabbath.

Meeting a Saint- 1992. When my French cousin called, excitedly inviting me to an afternoon Mass where Mother Teresa was to appear at the opening of one of her hospices for AIDS in downtown Baltimore, I initially balked. I didn't want the hassle of crowds and, besides, I had a funeral-wake service later that day. Eventually my cousin talked me into it.

Mother Teresa and author, FJL, at MC Motherhouse, Calcutta

Yes, I caved.

This choice changed my life.

In light of my challenge, here was The Plan: I'd go to Mass, hopefully see Mother Teresa, then leave for the wake service. Fine. So, as she entered St. Wenceslaus church for the mass, an electrifying spiritual vibrancy went through the congregation; everybody strained to get a look at her at this small, fragile-looking lady wearing a white-and-blue sari. She seemed strikingly luminescent. My boss, Archbishop Keeler, said the Mass. Mother Teresa sat in the front row and was praised by the prelate. She nodded humbly.

Later, when I left the church during the prayer of the faithful, as planned, I was stunned. My car was trapped in the middle of a dense metal forest of immoveable vehicles. I wasn't going anywhere. Time to panic? Well, yes. That lasted about a minute. Then I saw an official-looking man and asked him a question. Turned out he was an undercover policeman. As we talked, I learned he was Irish Catholic, and then mentioned my giant problem.

He had a solution! He'd give me a ride to the wake service in his police car! I thanked him profusely. Then I simply prayed my duty and bummed another ride back to St. Wenceslaus. Upon my return, I heard that Mother Teresa was meeting with officials of Johns Hopkins Hospital, along with my archbishop so, I decided to get into the rectory. Using the direct approach, and exuding confidence, I walked up to the entrance. Nobody stopped me. Good so far. I stuck my head through the doorway, stepped through, and saw a blue-and-white sari, a black-suited priest and other people sitting around a table. Everyone stared. Should I duck out? No, I decided, and to my amazement, Mother Teresa came to me, grasped my hand and smiled. I'd made it! I could breathe again. She greeted me warmly; I told her my name. Then she told me that she was thankful for priests, glimmering, and turned back to her meeting. Wow.

As if that wasn't enough, I began another vigil, and waited for her to emerge after all the meetings, with her sisters – I'd heard she would leave via a back door to a waiting van, for her return to New York.

She did, and once again, she came right up to me.

The Perfect Storm! I'd met a saint (again), asked for help, and told her I wanted to go on pilgrimage to India. Mother Teresa immediately said I *should* go, that I would be able to help her Missionary of Charity (MC) sisters, say Mass, and give talks to her sisters and retreat-attendees. She pointed to a nearby MC sister who would help me, my contact. It seemed so simple – too simple? It turned out to be the "the MC Way": minimize bureaucracy, maximize action. After I'd spoken with the contact, Mother Teresa took my right hand and taught me a prayer, consisting of five words.

With gnarled, bony little fingers, she emphasized each word of Jesus's admonition to help the poor, based on Matthew 25:40 (wherein Jesus implies His "visitations" upon earth as jailed, sick and poor persons), and just to *whom* one actually does it. Five words: "You-Did-It-To-*Me*". Mother Teresa tapped each of my fingers, pronounced each word on my hand with hers, each syllable emphasized, everything done consciously. What a moment!

I made my pilgrimage commitment right then, knowing a saint backed me!

LIFE LESSONS AND "PROPELLERS"

What did I learn from my Indian pilgrimage experiences that propelled me to take a group one more time?

Vigilance. In our fast-paced world, one doesn't want to wait needlessly. Vigilance, however, means being patient and to *practice* patience. Back in 1993 in India, I learned to wait and to savor each present moment, wherever I was. Remember Aesop's fable of the *Tortoise and the Hare*? The tortoise won that race; the dramatic hyper-hare burned out. So: *Be vigilant for your pilgrimage, wherever or whatever it is!*

Determination. *If you really want it!* This is one of the biggest lessons of life – cultivating-then-keeping that determination.

When I was a kid, I loved documentaries on TV about animals and travel, and always wondered what it would be like to actually go to these places – especially to such an exotic place like India. But inside, I thought: *Who are you kidding? You'll never get there.* Well, there's a saying: *As you think, so you do.* In my mind were pictures of the Taj Mahal, the slums of Calcutta, curried food and unusual people. Somehow, getting there had to be possible…

And then those connections opened, after that little talk with Mother Teresa. Other pilgrims I contacted responded, urged and surged, as did I.

We finally got there.

Now things seem so simple and possible, only because the groundwork had been laid. This time, I couldn't wait to return to India. For most people, I guess, it seems far away, exotic, a place for someone else to visit. Work with Mother Teresa? That's impossible. No, it *is* possible– well, it *was* possible for me. I did work with her back then, and still work with her sisters. And the place for that work was Calcutta – a place that's in a category by itself.

So: Desire it, visualize it, make "steppingstones". Realize them by following through. Imagine that desire, and keep it up.

Tenacity. Mother Teresa had the ability to totally focus. This was something I learned while working with her and her fellow nuns. Years later, that message and lesson still hold strong within me. My neighbor used an interesting word describing me once – *gumption*. It fits.

Right thinking. If you don't have it, you won't get it. *Huh*? If you don't have desires, goals or plans– and the ability to stick to those plans, you'll never arrive, achieve, or live a dramatic and adventure-filled life. A person needs desire and passion within one's body and soul to reach a desired destination. In my case, I had to keep that "right thinking" going – that I would make it to India.

Virtuous or venomous?

Fr. Lombardi and Irish seminarian volunteers he lived with one month

The thing you choose to think about, you'll do again and again. What you repeat becomes a habit. The habit becomes your inner life and eventually your character – which could be virtuous or venomous. Your character becomes your destiny. It all begins in one's head and, along with God, His Grace and His Providence, one must *choose* to think, live, love and learn. We disciples may become good or evil by the choices we make. Will you foster friendliness to God or frenzy and faithless fanaticism?

When I travelled to India in 1993, it was the end-result of a single mental obsession, well, that and my cousin inviting me to the Mass! I stayed focused, took advantage of opportunities *and* capitalized on them. So many things – from career choices, travel plans, recipes to healthy lifestyles – all begin in our minds and must be molded into daily practices.

Enjoying the ride. Whether taking planes, trains, buses or taxis while visiting various shrines in India, all of them gave me tons of experiences – mostly consisting of new-found encounters with myself and my Savior. Most of the time, I enjoyed them (some were arduous), took in everything around me, learned from those moment-to-moment experiences and surrendered to God. Very revealing, kind of like holy abandonment. In other words, brace oneself for Adventure!

As a novice pilgrim in 1993, and later in 2005 and 2009, I didn't always know what was going to happen on those trips, no matter how thorough my planning. Being in India can blur, change and spin one's plans, simply because of its myriad ways of, and spontaneous unfurling of life – India's pattern is not always aligned with the Western outlook on things. While there, be ready for anything, and know you'll have to adapt quickly. From my experiences, I've found the following qualities are useful: malleability, winess, spunkiness, gnarly tenacity, fortitude and zeal.

Toleration. Simply said, in India, you'll put up with a lot you're not used to. Try crowds, excessive heat and humidity, monsoons, possible sickness, waiting in chaotic lines, culinary challenges, pushy people, sacred cows running amok, and bathroom-shacks that are actually enclosures for a hole in the ground. I'm not kidding. Not to mention the constant changes to one's itinerary, or cancelled appointments. It will be up to the traveler whether to take it gracefully or not. My advice: Go with the pilgrimage flow!

Surprises. I expected a lot in incredible India. I carried within my mind so many varied images and stories, and the spiritual hopes while there. So, what did I experience on my first trip? Some experiences were good and, even, ecstatic, but there were disappointments: Bollywood-like gurus who crushed my philosophical aspirations, Hindu priests ripping off people, exacerbating poverty alongside upper crust folks who mistreated the lower castes, naked children washing in side-alleys, taxi drivers jacking up your fare, and street vendors constantly trying to negotiate a bargain. My illusions did not match reality, and I learned to take the bad with the good.

Longing for home. I had tons of fun during my 1993 Indian adventure, but there were times I couldn't wait to get back, usually generated when dealing with the inevitable heat, strange food, crowds, missing creature comforts and familiar surroundings. That's part of travel. You enjoy being there but still miss home.

As much as these and other Indian stories are like life in general, sometimes life is NOT like that. Some experiences in India were totally different and *un*like anything in the West. It's at those times when such experiences can reveal something about you, the world and God, which aren't repeatable anywhere else.

What's the most obvious about India? Crowds. Masses of people everywhere – streets, buses, taxis, plazas, train stations, intersections, airplane terminals, tourist shops, even at lemonade stops. India teems with people– surging throngs, and everyone's in a hurry. Indians are not shy about pushing into your personal space! So, knowing all this, I sometimes asked myself late in 2008: *How can I go through that again?*

Socialization versus individualization. Generally speaking, the West is more individualistic than the East – which tends to be more communal in outlook. I've found this to be very apparent on my visits to not only India, but Africa, also.

While on our 2009 trip, we made a mini-pilgrimage to a shrine – Our Lady the Virgin – and I had a good talk with a fellow pilgrim during our rather-bumpy ride. She'd lived in India for a year, and shared with me this difference between East and West.

Basically, India is "public"–in that many things are done in the open: Sleeping, shaving, showering, cleaning, washing clothes, bargaining, teaching. There are rarely any closed doors in India, nor is there an expectation of privacy. Other examples: Extreme poverty – whether it be bathroom amenities (or lack thereof), poor-quality clothes to no clothing, lack of food, no modern conveniences. There's a reason it's called—or was— the "third world".

Harsh beauty. Those are words I'd use to describe the Lord Jesus. Think of His poverty, His self-denial, His heroic-sacrificial love by carrying the Cross to a bitter death. Harsh beauty also describes the Gospel – the apostles' simplicity, ruggedness and martyrdom. Harsh beauty also describes priests, nuns and lay people who deny themselves, and noble missionaries eaten by lions. Christianity and life are each a grab-bag of joy and sorrow, which seems like an oxymoron, but is a reality of life. In life, there is obviously harshness and there is beauty. India is no exception and, in fact, is probably the epitome of it.

Perhaps you've heard of the movie *Slumdog Millionaire*. Well, some movies you go *to*, others you go *through*. After my recent pilgrimage to India, this movie captivated me; I saw it two weeks after my 2009 trip. It was as if I was right back in India. The movie is about survival and healing. The story-line: Two Muslim boys are thrown into the chaos of Mumbai (Bombay), following their family's persecution and obliteration. The boys' survival is depicted as dramatic, comedic, but always adventurous. They become street entrepreneur-opportunists, eventually professional beggars (unwittingly), worked for a crime outfit, until their maturation unto adulthood, which brings on the climax of the movie. One boy eventually entered an Indian "I Want to Be A Millionaire" show, and by flashbacks to his childhood, provided providentially-good answers to questions. The other boy embraced crime, yet eventually turned good. At the end, almost all India awaits the "slumdog" (term for beggar-entrepreneurs) good boy's answer in the game show. It's a perfect storm of an ending. Rags to riches? See for yourself.

Like a pilgrimage to India, this movie was sensual, sometimes assaulting, interactive and contained low-to-high adrenalin pumping intoxication. It's a path through another land, and ultimately through yourself. And if you do go to India, just like watching the movie, you'll need a sense of adventure and fortitude, and a strong stomach!

GETTING AWAY/BREAKING AWAY…
Translation: You Don't Know What You're Missing!

Ever notice? Sometimes it's hard to get away. Whether it's a day off from work, going on vacation or retreat – things in life pile up, demand attention, but still, you must pack and go. There are many important things to do. Some are un-important. Sometimes we cave and do the unimportant anyway, and keep putting off getting away. In the Gospel, Jesus bemoans this attitude when he says "Let the dead bury their dead" (Lk. 9:60). Hyperbole? Yes, a little. Truth? Yes, that too. Jesus also says, "Whoever wishes to come after me must deny himself, take up his cross, and follow me" (Mt. 16:24). Translation: The time to act is now! Getting overburdened by life, possessions, people—it's a struggle.

My process in trip planning, whether long or short: I try to set aside time for it, make an effort, all the while knowing (hopefully not sabotaging myself) that I'm ignoring a pile of things-to-do: Making calls, answering emails, packing, checking and changing schedules. Sometimes I can leave on time. Mostly I don't. I do try to avoid the extreme of being an hour late but sometimes it happens.

While I certainly don't want to make it seem that our 2009 pilgrimage was the Most Excellent Adventure Ever, I will stress that it was one of most-fun things I've ever done in life (besides surfing, maybe). Some people have very important reasons not to travel: lack of money, work demands, family responsibilities. Other people might say going to India isn't sensible. Really? However, if they knew what they'd be missing, would they make another choice? Maybe?

There are those who stay home because it's simple and uncomplicated. Yes, travel means complexity, generates possible risk to life and limb, but the knowledge and experience gained far outweigh the risk. Avid travelers (like me) are risk-takers who happily seek adventures and *make things happen*. In my experience, everyone who pilgrimages has a blast!

SO… WHY TRAVEL IN THE FIRST PLACE?

After many postings as a priest over central and Western Maryland, I've learned a great deal–things I might not have learned had I stayed in one place. So, willingly or not, through various assignments I have personally grown by *detaching* myself from familiar surroundings, family and friends, rather than becoming entrenched in what I see as the typical parish life of priesthood and ministry.

I also learned how small the world is after travelling and that it seems to get smaller with familiarity. Ever notice when you go to a new place, the initial journey there seems overly long, but the return is short? When I was once assigned to Cumberland –in western Maryland, nearly three hours' drive from Baltimore – it felt like I'd moved to Alaska; the drive took "forever". But after making that trip several times, it was a snap, as if space had seemingly collapsed between Cumberland and Baltimore.

Then I was assigned to Hancock, a town in the narrowest part of Maryland, west of Hagerstown and east of Cumberland. People in Baltimore said Hancock was too far west, in the boonies, out-of-the-way; my reaction to this? Mostly neutral, as I realized these people had never lived anyplace else. This proves the great value of travel, that it makes one a "citizen of the world," providing opportunities to learn about different cultures, peoples, lifestyles, and that thru this expressed in diverse ways.

As a potential traveler-pilgrim, you may find it necessary to avoid some common extremes, such as *provincialism,* which preaches your home place is the only game in the global town. Rather than being so insular, embrace the different-ness of people, their cultures and geography. All these things can help you like your hometown-gig, but at the same time, it teaches you to appreciate God's creativeness while whetting your appetite for seeing and experiencing more of His world.

I think of my dad—he has never been on an airplane, never been out of the country. He likes his tomato plants, daily newspaper and simple, homespun life. Somehow, I came from him and yet I love to travel. We're opposites in some ways, yet we two are part of God's Mystical Body. So, I shall recommend this: Do your homework. Learn how to travel; learn about India in all of its glory and challenges; expand your cultural view, but increase thankfulness for your own upbringing. Learn the smells and bells of India and elsewhere. They're an amalgamation of joy and sorrow, like life.

ROMANTICISM VS. REALISM

Everyone dreams of travelling – sometimes to exotic places like Bali, New Zealand, or Kashmir. If that's your dream, then India is not the location you want! Along these lines regarding vacation/pilgrimage, be ready! You won't get familiar food; it might be hot, spicy, very-foreign and probably not to your taste. That's reality. Realism is needed here, not romanticism.

The same reality-check should apply to lodgings. An Indian hotel might be more like a hostel or a shared dormitory room. In other words, it's not Club Med. An Indian pilgrimage is just the opposite, just as Outward Bound is the opposite of an all-expense-paid easy ride. So then, this present adventure account may, unfortunately, remain largely in your head, but, hopefully, because of my "Life Is Like That" theme, there might be some parts of this book that will resonate within you.

As you read further on, consider these questions:

- How can this Indian storyline and adventure transform my life?
- How can this account help me to love God, my neighbors, friends and family?
- How can I cannot relate to a particular story to an aspect of my life or someone else's to grow in wisdom and spirutality?

So, enjoy the ride ahead, and let it inspire you to see some strange land far away. Nothing is impossible. Keep dreaming.

CHAPTER 2

*"All blessings come to us through our Lord.
He will teach us, for in beholding his life
we find that he is the best example."*
–St. Teresa of Avila

Spirituality, Theology and God

*"The most deadly poison of our times is indifference.
And this happens, although the praise of God
should know no limits. Let us strive, therefore, to
praise him to the greatest extent of our powers."*
-Maximillion Kolbe

I once met a priest who immediately reminded me of God, and wholeness of life!

It was at a retreat designed for priests. I saw this man, figured from his appearance he was from India, and had to meet him. After slightly bowing, making the traditional Indian posture of folded hands at my forehead, and saying *Namaste,* we introduced ourselves. His name was Father Devia, and apparently, *Devia* means God! Fantastic. He was from Goa, in southern India, where I had once visited way back, and we talked about the beaches there – where we'd both gone swimming, I, as a visitor in 1993, and he, of course, as a local. Then I asked him what exactly *namaste* meant, since I had heard several interpretations. His answer: "It means, 'I honor God in you'..." Nice.

As we spoke further, Father Devia then said that India is a spiritual place and I wholeheartedly agreed. He also said India breathes spirit and soul from ancient times to today, and I immediately understood, as that spirituality was why I'd gone there in the first place. It felt good to meet this man, and I was once again reminded of my Indian experience.

A local Hindu shrine in countryside

I once saw a travel advertisement, *Incredible India*. Catchy, yes, and true! India *is* incredible, very spiritual. Father Devia and I recalled the Ganesha – tiny long-trunked elephant god-statues in taxis, Hindu temples and street-corner shrines, Christian churches burning incense, Muslim and Hindu calls to prayer in the evenings, flower-petal offerings heaped around street-vendor stalls, nuns in habits of all descriptions, wandering monks and Hindu *om* symbols. Religion and spirituality are part of India. They *are* India. Incredibly so.

In a different way, America is also a spiritual place, based on polls and reports of how many people believe in God, go to church and pray regularly. We *are* a religious nation, but not overtly so. India's spirituality is indigenous and external, very open in its various forms, compared to the more-internal and privately-expressed spiritual leanings in America. Our culture has its dark and light sides, as does India's. Changing our environs to make them more spiritual? That's a big job, whether in America or India.

SPIRITUALITY… In the world religions

For orthodox Catholics who love their faith, and who are possibly interested in India or things eastern, this question comes up: If India has all that spirituality and religion, as the oldest, and most enduring in the world, is Indian culture – and Hinduism in particular – wrong or harmful? Hmmm. Very good question, and here are some of *my* answers:

1-The Catholic Church teaches that there are seeds of truth in every religion, germinating but not fully realized, and yet are not the total truth. Natural law pervades all. In other words, the wish to do good – and avoid evil, and seek the "Supreme" – has been placed by God in everyone's heart.

2-There are "errors" in other religions. *What*? you may ask. Well, there *is* the Indian caste system which oppresses and stigmatizes so many. And then one of the most confusing errors? Gods, so many of them, one can't figure out the differences between them and the purposes of each. And think of all the sacrifices to these gods. You may read Vatican Council II's document, *Nostra Aetaete*, on non-Christian religions, on this matter.

Enlightenment, a buzzword one hears in New-Age groups, it can sometimes be a ticket to self-absorption or over-distortion of individualization, but it is not a way to worship God. It's far more important to honor God rather than winning liberation or supposedly waking up – whatever that really means.

And the major error I see is *monism*, which by definition means there is no separate creation or Creator – there is no division between God and creatures, nor are there real individuals within the so-called creation, no parts of any whole. On the surface, at least to me, it seems rather nebulous and non-specific, devoid of spirituality.

Further, Eastern morality is created by mortals, which is not based on any metaphysical foundation, since there is no revelation, "Revealer" or creator (as there is in Christianity).

While there are many differences between our religions – which are unbridgeable – there *are* many similarities. *What?* you may ask. Well, most Indian religions believe in a particular, individual judgment after death, albeit in different ways. We both believe in forms of morality; we are called to an ethical quest and lifestyle to something higher. There are sacrifices, a priesthood, and worship. Monastic traditions exist, too, in both religions, and we have specially set-aside places and communities for the pursuit of God, spirituality and higher things. Meditation and contemplation are universal attributes of all religions. Interdependence exists as well, a common thread of religions means one thing affects many other things.

Just like anything else in religious matters, we need balance. We, as representatives of Hinduism and Catholicism, should talk and be amenable on what we can agree and, conversely, determine on what we disagree, while embodying charity in all things. There's a lot to be gained from religious dialogue. and as we gained in our pilgrimage serving in the environment of others in great need, it helped transform, broaden and deepen our own spiritual paths.

I recall a conversation/dialogue of sorts back in 1993 with a group of Indian men. They were flabbergasted that I was a celibate priest, as in actually not married. They honored me, but couldn't understand, and kept asking: *Why are you not with a lady?* So, we sat under tall trees in the Indian sunset and rapped about philosophy, God and truth, but still, there was their wonderment. *Wow. You don't have a wife!* They thought it kind of great, as in a sacrifice, a concept they could understand and appreciate.

RIPPED-OFF ROSARY AND REASONABLENESS

Here are some conclusions I've reached visiting India and studying eastern spirituality:

While there are good, evocative things and many learnable lessons in India, what you envision doesn't always match reality. I once thought of all Indians as "spiritualists", because, after all, they're Indians. Now I think of most of them as revered inheritors of a classic spiritual tradition.

And there's a whole industry here in the West which prizes and projects Things Eastern to the heights of adulation. Reasons for this are many (rejection of things western, infatuation complex, exotica, etc.). This industry feeds the American mind (as it did mine in the past) and people subsequently can lose the power of making subtle distinctions and using spiritual discretion.

There's truth in the East, but you don't always see it lived. Of all places, India is a land and pilgrimage of truth. And yet oppositely, I remember getting pickpocketed while on a bus in Calcutta and ripped off enroute to the Buddha's shrine. Contradictions exist everywhere; you have to watch your pockets and evade gangs even at ground-zero of Christendom, in St. Peter's square in Rome!

There are outright contradictions and contrariness in other cultures and religions. I got my newly bought – and prized – Buddhist rosary ripped off once in Tibet, of all places. I remember people treating me badly while riding trains and buses in India. Lesson learned from that: The grass *isn't* always greener on the other side of the planet, as I once dreamed it might be. At one time, I thought of India as a meditative place (people doing all kinds of lotus positions), but realized that for the most part, India was frenetic, noisy, and for the most part *not* meditative.

You may project onto the "other," as in your hosts in-country, when you are dreamy-eyed and mystified. I used to think of most Indians as somehow enlightened and pacified and, obviously, not all Indians are this way – just as all Catholics are not saints.

What I found in life is that when you encounter the "real thing," hopefully, you can make a clear and sober judgment about it. Indians and eastern spirituality are no different.

While I have grown more realistic about India and eastern spiritualities, my new conclusion is this: The "truth lies in the middle". One can find and embrace perennial truths and spiritual practices in varied places all the while realizing there are many possible errors that one cannot wipe away.

SPIRITUAL PATHS WHILE "IN-COUNTRY"

Why do I like going to India? Because it makes me feel spiritual, and I think of God frequently – it's not hard. There are so many reminders of God (sometimes beguiling ones). Also, I go with other people who pray a lot. While there, you need God quite a bit – you're far away from home and there are lots of people who don't look like you, with the realization that *you* are the alien standing out in the crowd, naturally, you *will* pray.

In 2005, as a small group of pilgrims in-country of USA, we celebrated Mass and recited the Rosary. We prayed the liturgy of hours (Psalms and Bible readings). We made pilgrimages to religious shrines. And there are reminders all over India that you are not just a materialist cog, but a spiritual soul.

In the U.S., I need to think of God very actively, and must do it quite a bit. Sure, there is always the occasional church one might see on the corner as a kind of "epiphany", in small towns or the countryside, but through so many offensive reminders in our culture (abrasive commercials, sensual ways of dressing; outright materialism, etc.), you always have to urge yourself to think about God. In India, on the other hand, the country itself continuously reminds you of God. When many Indians would see me on the street wearing a cross, crucifix, or Roman collar, they honored me – they made a salutation to me, acknowledging God. *They* reminded me of God.

There's a book, called *Karma Cola,* by Gita Mehta, that is an excellent revelation which describes the false images of eastern religions, and subtitled, "Marketing the Mystic East." As in: the "saffron robe syndrome," exotic places, burning incense (specifically the patchouli westerners get into). Yes, the Taj Mahal is great and so is Kashmir and Himalayan ashram-enlightenment centers, and the semi-socialistic primal communities which are evocative. Eastern mystique is gripping many, but don't get blindsided. India really *is* incredible, but go there enlightened!

"I'm spiritual but not religious"… Some time ago, this phrase appeared in social media, gained in popularity, and mainstreamed for a while, especially among celebrities—and our family members. It does seem to be heard nowadays in the U.S. But when you think about this seeming contradiction-in-terms, you may (hopefully) ask this question: *What gave spirituality to us in the first place?* Answer: It was religion itself. Spirituality didn't – couldn't – develop totally divorced from religion, so, assume this supposed separation-concept has validity, and is harmful thinking to a true spiritual seeker. Religion and spirituality *can* and *do* go together, especially within Catholic Christianity.

During my 1993 Indian pilgrimage, I went to the famous burning ghats of Varanasi, on the Ganges River. When I walked by the river, I viewed those ominous funeral pyres from a distance, with attendant men burning piled-up bodies. Yes, I was there on purpose, as I'd read about this in *National Geographic*. The reality was different. It was unbelievably hot (middle of summer, no air conditioning, no fresh water for swimming, and barely a shower at our sanctuary).

I thought then and there about reincarnation. Hindus believe that the spirit or *atman* (defined as true self, or soul) of a person which survives death will return to another body of life until it is finally purified of all defilement and karma, free and totally pure.

The teaching of reincarnation may be deplorable in many ways (like eternal recurrence of the same soul, the caste system, legalism, etc.) but there is still fascination regarding reincarnation's stress on purification from sin and renewal of the soul. However, I can't imagine that a personal Intelligence or Lord would send a human back as a cricket, tree or sea mollusk. But… I'm thinking Hindus are on to something, as in purification of human imperfection and the "payment" for one's deeds. This is one of those aforementioned "seeds of truth" which would seem to be germinating but is not yet fully-flowered, or able to be expressive of total truth. (As an aside, one could further observe that reincarnation could be used as a system of serfdom control and manipulation.)

Here are two burning questions. 1) Who is making up the grid for moral determination (what is right and wrong), and 2) Who gets re-birthed?

Another critique of "Western-Eastern" infatuation: there is a changing of, or even an overthrow of the western ethical system. In other words, the "East becomes West" trend has become so Americanized and sterilized (in other words, "de-religioned") it has already lost its essence. These proponents see Christianity as smothering and "old world" and want to promote anything against it. Hinduism is seen as sophisticated, exotic and trendy – so, who can be against all that?

GOD-QUEST, OR DIVINE APPEARANCES

Our lives are both a *quest for*, and *encounter of*, God. Our lives should also be an announcement of Him to others. Or, actually, it should be a *reminder* to others about their "first Love", to see God (Rev. 2:4). When seen in retrospect, my 2005 pilgrimage to India was like a *documentation of Divinity* – encountering the Lord both mysteriously and magnificently through prayer, fellowship and in new ways, thereby deepening our soul-lives through explicit and subtle experiences.

Case in point. I recall the singing at Mother Teresa's Motherhouse and how it instantly reminded me of God – it put me in His presence and inspired me. Let's just say that hearing two hundred nuns singing to God gets into your sinews and has a lasting effect.

God made us for Him. "Our hearts are ever restless until they rest in Thee, O God..." St. Augustine famously prayed. That expresses something we feel and think of as a sentiment, because God has placed this longing within us. God put in our DNA the capacity to seek Him. Christian-Catholics see this as a marvelous oneness, after all, we are from God (our souls were made out of nothing by Him), therefore, we seek Him and our Homeland, our true Origin.

So, then, our goal should be simple, that is, life equals God.

I shall propose a question. *What is the goal of a pilgrimage?* Is the answer God? A pilgrimage helps us to encounter Him – and life – in a new way, deepening our soul-lives, all while having a good time and interesting adventures. Whether through prayer, work or serving others, there are many "faces" of God, and so many ways to encounter Him. Gradually, we are able to see those various faces. Opportunities to do so can occur poignantly, sometimes surprisingly, during a pilgrimage.

Like a many-faceted diamond, there are different aspects of God. Sometimes He is clear and immediately-revealing, and at other times, He is hidden and seemingly anonymous. Similarly, on pilgrimage, you may have sudden up-experiences, and just as quickly things can crash into struggle and pain. Roller coasters exist everywhere, even within our bodies and souls!

Sometimes you may encounter God close to home – maybe while performing daily duties or during a commute. For some, encountering God doesn't happen until one is far from home – in another culture and among strangers. In our travels to India, we encountered God in those many different people. Some were happy, while others were destitute and obviously suffering, but God's face was evident within all – showing us why we came to India in the first place.

India is the birthplace of Hinduism – which is a whole lesson of learning and pilgrimage in itself, and this oldest of religions now influences much of the New-Age movement in the West.

By way of definition, Hinduism is an amalgamation of spiritualities, and to many in the West, this is especially beguiling. I heard a comment once from a fellow pilgrim years ago, that Hinduism is both *flexible* and *shrewd*. It can absorb and integrate almost any spirituality in the world, even as it retains itself – and is able to encompass the "new" into its "old". For instance, as part of this spiritual syncretism, Jesus is portrayed as both God and an avatar of the Ultimate Being. So, in this view, Christ is accepted, and at the same time neutralized by Hinduism's multiple aspects. New-Age is basically a grab-bag of "east-meets-west" spiritualities; *monism* is rather pervasive. Western influence manifests in some form of pop psychology that constantly refers back to the Self.

But here's an irony. Hinduism largely rejects the concept of self as we understand it.

And, have you noticed there's a good bit of yoga around? This is largely the influence of Hinduism. Yoga is promoted in Fortune 500 companies, at retreats, PTA meetings and community centers for exercise. As long as exercise is the primary focus, then this is acceptable to serious Christian-Catholics. Incorporating meditation, or other-spiritual segments into the sessions should raise a red flag, however. Enough said.

MISSIONARIES OF CHARITY SPIRITUALITY

Mother Teresa's "First Love" and care facility established in Calcutta, previously a Hindu temple

One thing you'll notice after a while in India, is that nearly all the Missionaries of Charity(called MCs) look the same. Most post-moderns might dislike this at first glance, after all, everybody looks cut from the same boring mold. But, reality is very different. Yes, the sisters dress alike, but in their demeanors, these ladies are not boring at all. Whether young or old, they are steady, cheerful and, most of all —they are all about God! Most of them came from poor backgrounds, have all kinds of challenges living amidst the worst poverty anywhere, but they do daily chores, conduct common *and* private prayer sessions many times of the day. They clean their environs, work with the poorest of the poor, and yet the MCs continue to be happy and genuinely light-filled.

Most people are happy only if they are comfortable, and get what they want. By contrast, MCs are zealous and elated while serving in slums, living in poverty, eating gruel and living literally on the equivalent of ten cents a day. The perceived "MC cookie-cutter-syndrome" is especially noticeable in their giggling laughs; the ladies cheer up while talking about the Mass, and their love for Mother Teresa, (who they call Mother). And yes, they are the same in their serenity, their service and their naïveté.

Many MCs are friendly, smiling and approachable; sometimes they are satirical and ironic. You may talk to an MC for a while, and become friendly, but know this: she will always be a lover of the Lord. MCs sleep in dorms, do piles of laundry, and sometimes go on retreats. But always, they put God first and then the poor, then the Eucharist and, following, their simplicity of life.

We pilgrims learned from the MCs, and were inspired by their love of God and the poor, a significant lesson we can apply not only to the goal of our pilgrimage, but to our lives as well!

LOVE

Through India, some western souls may give in to the lure of the Buddha, the saffron robes, Hinduism's begging monks, and so forth. To be fair, many of us in the West have neglected and rejected the contemplative culture of our Catholic Faith, promoted originally by medieval monastics, but seems to be severely demoted in importance today, supplanted by too much time on mobile computing devices to the point of addiction. Many pay the price for this neglect – fragmentation of the soul.

Many people, including myself years ago, flew East to find inner peace, to then realize –ironically – it was already present in the West. I found it was possible to become a contemplative soul within my own Catholic culture, that I could become enlightened and freed from the frenzy of life.

Given all the above, we need to admit something: The Buddha didn't do it; neither did Mohammad, Confucius or Plato. But: Jesus *did*. He gave up His life by dying for us! Jesus loved us so much He wanted us to *continue* to experience what love is – by His own radical example. In St. John's gospel, Jesus gave two radical sayings: "As the Father has loved Me, so I love you…This I command you: Love one another" (Jn.15: 9-17). The *infinite love* God the Father has for His Son is passed on from Jesus to us!

If Buddhism and Hinduism are more about enlightenment, then Christianity is more about love (to exaggerate a bit). Eastern religions are more about personal liberation; Christianity is about loving bunches of people. Most of our pilgrims would admit this. They were going to India because of love, as in loving others through service. We had seen pictures and films of Mother Teresa and her sisters feeding the poor. They were going because of Love of God – discovering Him in another place; love was the motive for travelling with other pilgrims, finding God in each other and in our communal bonds.

The point?

Well, it *is* about love. That love is a Person, in Jesus. Knowing and loving Him is all about an encounter with Him in a living relationship.

In India, we loved going to Mass and praying with the MCs at the Motherhouse, as this fronted the rest of our day. Same for our evening prayers, and performing night holy hours at the Motherhouse. We wanted and lived out this relationship in daily ways by our encounter with God in prayer and spiritual practices.

GO WITH GOD

The main purpose of our pilgrimage in 2009 was not sightseeing, discovering a new culture, expanding our horizons or even serving others. It was about honoring God – and this came through seeing God's beauty in His creation, finding Him in a different land and serving others – that is, God first and His creation second!

There are many forms of worship, of course, but our pilgrimage-goal was to worship God in an exciting country, have new personal service encounters by imitating a saint, Mother Teresa, and, most especially, by being open to God's glory and revelations. God *is* the prism through which we see and experience all reality.

One of my favorite mantras comes from the Jesuits: *Finding God in all things*. This Jesuit motto helps directs the mind and will within a given endeavor to encounter God, leaving no event out of the realm of God's revelation. We had all kinds of opportunities to practice this, I must say!

Were we nervous? Of course. Some of the usual challenges to be nervous about? There was serious air pollution; dealing with a daily language barrier; and avoiding sacred cows, among many other things. But we all decided this: *Go with God, find Him in all places and situations.* We abandoned ourselves and made a choice for spiritual elation by encountering the new, the different and the bold. Going with God means, as St. Francis de Sales said, "God who kept you yesterday and keeps care of you today will be the same God who takes care of you tomorrow, Who is there before you get there…" And so, yes, we found God where we were, even it was challenging.

We all get nervous and anxious about life and unpredictable situations. When I received an assignment to Cumberland, in western Maryland, it seemed like I was moving to another planet – so different than being in Baltimore. THE biggest help to me was this saying by St. Francis. It calmed my mind. After a short time, I felt right at home, peaceful and grateful

Here's another saying that helps me by Meister Eckhart, a 13th-century German theologian: "God is the being Whose center is everywhere and Whose circumference is nowhere." When we are truly present in our surroundings, fully in "the skin" of our culture, then we can *experience* God – not simply find Him.

We all need to take steps to this conversion of essentially *being where we are*. Frederick Matthews Green likes to say: "Everyone wants to be transformed, but no one wants to change." Well, that's true. We want dramatic transformation and integration into Christ and all that, buuuuut, we don't want to take the small, hard and necessary steps to bring this about.

Just as a mighty waterfall begins miles before as a little stream, we need to begin simply, and keep going, and to think big. Provincialism – thinking only your hometown/village/culture is everything – promotes small-mindedness, and crushes a desire for discovery and adventure. After my many postings and associated travel, I've grown to love, accept and benefit from all my assignments which free me, although they started out as quite challenging! And so, as we made pilgrimage to India, we learned how to grow out of our Western "skins" into new, Eastern ones, and found God there.

SACRED HEART

In Matthew's gospel, Jesus says, *"Come to Me all you who are burdened and I will give you rest"* (11:28). My friend, (and now, I trust, in Heaven) Deacon Vince Perticone said this was one of the greatest verses in the Bible. This verse reminds me of – and can be related to – the Sacred Heart statues we sometimes see in our churches and icons. They depict Jesus, usually with His arms extended into the air, robes flowing beneath Him, and a heart aflame in the center of His chest, with a crown of thorns around it. Some of these statues and pictures are appealing to some, after all, Jesus has warm feelings, is aflame for us, and so we humans can approach Him as Divinity. He is open to us and all people. Jesus is a real human being, and God, albeit with a supernatural heart for souls.

When we visited various chapels in Calcutta and Darjeeling, we saw a lot of those Sacred Heart statues. They were often at the front entrance of schools and convents, as if to greet us. I was struck by their seeming-omnipresence in the Indian Catholic community, begun by Jesuit missionaries in the sixteenth century, demonstrating great devotion to the Lord and His Sacred Heart and spread this wherever they went – to great effect with shrewd practicality.

So, what about us? We, as individuals, can make an enthronement to the Sacred Heart – dedicate oneself, home and family and all who enter and visit – to Jesus. We have football flags and signs for our favorite teams. Why not celebrate the Lord Jesus more through the Sacred Heart?

> **Aspiration…**
>
> **Fire within/Breathe Him…**
>
> Imagine the fiery Spirit of Jesus within you. This fire ascends and descends through your body, swirling around your heart. Make Jesus Christ personal – breathe Him within, through your body and soul. Everything is now Light-filled and irradiated by His enflaming Love.

DIVINITY

The word comes from Latin –*divinitas,* in some contexts, meaning to foresee (as well as being God-like). That is the essence of divinity, and if you think about it, what we humans might want in life – the ability to know and see everything before it happens. God sees all-at-once; meanwhile, we finite creatures cannot. But, realistically, would it actually help to see and view everything all at once? Some would immediately say YES! It would alleviate a lot of suffering and learning by increments. Others say NO! For one thing, we couldn't take so much information and challenges at one time; it would overwhelm us. Besides, life without surprises? How boring.

Well, as they say about India and pilgrimages: Expect the unexpected! When we were planning our pilgrimage, there were so many questions to answer first. Which airline? How many seats? What to pack? Which hotel? Should we spend time in recreation or service? Should we make a schedule for each day? And so forth…

Plan as much as you can, given what the knowledge you possess; somehow, you learn to be open and resilient regarding upcoming surprises, and enjoy the rest, especially during pilgrimage.

We made good decisions – staying at the Our Lady Seven Dolors parish was a great base of operations, with secure lodgings, good food, and hospitable people. We also made bad decisions – for instance, spending too many days in Darjeeling in lodgings that were frigid and musty – bad for health and morale, so we made up for it and left the mountains to spend more time in Calcutta, serving. Our youth especially liked that!

Looking back at our planning process, in general, it was done blindly, but we were thankful nonetheless – that no matter how things happened, nobody was maimed or left behind. We made the best of our situations, and realized that what we'd done, seen and had gone through together was truly a spiritual adventure.

While on this kind of adventure, a pessimist would get stuck on minor details, perhaps get bogged down, or become depressed. But a realist rolls with the punches. One tour director once said, "You can make knee-jerk observations while on pilgrimage, and become susceptible to over-generalization. That's when you remind yourself to look at the overall picture and not sweat the small stuff…" Amidst the challenges, it means learning to absorb bad things and move on. Stick with your plan as much as practical, but be flexible.

PRAYER

Before leaving the States on pilgrimage, we said a prayer, forming a circle and holding hands in Dulles International Airport. Yes, it felt a little strange praying amidst bustling travelers, but that's why we were there, to be about God, to pray and offer our time and talents to Him. How much can a person pray in one day? We have all kinds of attractions and distractions, some good, and some bad. It's hard to pray, not to mention maintain focus and foster an interior life. It's hard enough getting through life in one's own backyard, but we were about to thrive and survive on a pilgrimage in a strange land. At that moment, in the airport terminal, we consciously committed ourselves to the Lord, and forged within ourselves union with one another and with God. This became the most common element of our pilgrimage.

As a common-sense person once said: "How can you have communion without communication?" If you want to talk to your friend (not using a phone or carrier pigeon) you have to actually talk to them!

We prayed in all kinds of situations: On a train overnight to Darjeeling, in a train station thick with pickpockets and entrepreneurs, at hotels while stuck for another unplanned day in India. We prayed in church quarters, waiting at airport terminals, in moving SUVs, in crowded buses and taxis, while walking to ministry work on the dark streets of Calcutta. And just about every morning and night, we prayed the Liturgy of the Hours, celebrated Mass and prayed the Rosary together. Some fell asleep during these times, as it was so peaceful and we were often exhausted. It was common for some to zone out right away; others would just sit and stare, while others were wide awake and led the charge.

Prayer can be challenging. In Darjeeling during our 2005 pilgrimage, we made holy hour – a daily activity, praying before the Blessed Sacrament, but this time, it was freezing. There was no indoor heating in the Jesuit house where we stayed. We wore hats, gloves and heavy coats in chapel; our breaths were visible in the frosty air. One thing was certain: no one fell asleep! It was a reminder that this was a pilgrimage, not a religious tour, and to get used to the rhythm of regular, daily prayer.

Praying at Mother Teresa's Tomb. It was the first day after arrival and recuperation from our night flight. We went to Mother Teresa's Motherhouse. It is a long, clean building inside and out, in downtown Calcutta. For many in our pilgrimage group, this was a high point – being at "spiritual ground zero" where a saint was buried. When everyone walked into the simple chapel (no fancy fanciness here!), you then realized the chapel is literally a few scant feet from a major road. Everyone immediately zeroed in on her tomb – a large concrete, yellowish-painted crypt with statue of the Virgin Mary on it and child Jesus joyfully reaching out. There is a plaque with Mother Teresa's favorite Bible verse: "Love one another as I have loved you" (Jn. 13:34).

We pilgrims then knelt on a stone floor near the tomb, hearing cars and busses whizzing outside. There was restrained joy all around – we had made it! So, we prayed in silence and stood, visited outside in the nearby courtyard, then prepared for Mass next door.

Although poignant for me, the pilgrims' fresh and enthusiastic encounter helped remind me of the treasure I had just tasted and to not take it for granted.

This spirituality and attempts at regular prayer werefor us a combination of St. Ignatius's admonitions: "Finding God in all things" and to do "mindfulness prayer". There's a Latin maxim: *age quod ageis,* meaning "Do what you are doing". We were challenged to keep an awareness of God while also learning from and appreciating the unique, unrepeatable uniqueness of this sacred encounter.

While in India, we pilgrims visited men with AIDS and tuberculosis in a Jesuit hospice one night. After touring the personal rooms, we gathered several clients outside on a veranda. They did not express themselves, as the obvious communication gap thing was strong. Plus, we couldn't discern much about their likes and dislikes. As it was the Christmas season, we sang *Silent Night*. All the men looked up at us, humbly and profoundly, some with tears in their eyes. They folded their hands and enjoyed the music in sacred silence. We could see on their sorrowful-yet-dignified faces the appreciation they had for us and the sacredness of the song, even though they could not understand a word. All of us felt the immediacy and depth of their thankfulness, all without speaking. It was worth the trip to India just for that. We left with the hope we had planted within their souls the love of Jesus and healing peace.

Missionary of Charity Motherhouse stairwell
where all volunteers would pass daily

Concentration. I'm always impressed by the Missionaries of Charity sisters, especially when they pray at the Motherhouse chapel, at night and in the morning. They are in complete attentiveness to Our Lord. When praying at night, they usually kneel looking up at the altar or the crucifix or Sacred Eucharist. Thing is, it's noisy: Pilgrims coming and going, cars and buses honking outside, people yelling, birds flying near the windows; attendants helping appoint the altar. *I* was certainly distracted, *BUT,* and this is a biggie, the MC sisters weren't. They were totally focused on Someone higher. Their attentiveness is almost miraculous, demonstrating absolute fixation – the epitome of spiritual life.

According to Mother Teresa, this is what gives the sisters fuel: seeing Christ in His Real Presence in the Sacred Eucharist – empowering them to attend the poorest of the poor. Along these lines, I recall well when Mother Teresa gave me a copy of her little booklet of prayer, *I Thirst*, which has a passionate picture of Jesus on the cover. As I read, I was enthralled, as this was actually, originally, a letter from Mother to her "daughters" – about her urgency to truly encounter Jesus in life, in the prayer life *and* in the Eucharist, not just inside the head. So often we can think about Jesus and put it on "automatic pilot" – basically sailing along on past fumes of spiritual life and then fail to encounter Him again in daily life. Mother Teresa reminded her sisters – and me – that we are not part of an ideology, but of a Jesus-movement and that we need to constantly meet Him in chapel and on the streets.

So, based on the above, is *this* why Calcutta is so popular with Westerners? Because of Mother Teresa's devotion to Jesus while alive – in the Eucharist and in the poor? After all, this is what led her to service. We're describing, in this book, how *Life is Like That*, as when one thing leads to another. Mother's love of Jesus led to her love of Him in the poor, which led us and thousands of others to Calcutta. We were attracted by serving and loving others, and found it led to love itself, Jesus Christ.

Austere Beauty. Those are the words I often recollect, when describing the Missionaries of Charity Chapel in Calcutta. The chapel is simple, threadbare – monastic, cell-like and minimalistic. Obviously, Mother Teresa didn't want her sisters to get off-track, so, I'll give you a "Just the basics, please" description. Their chapel includes a crucifix of Jesus in agony in the center – life-size and bloody. To one side of the altar is a tall, elegant statue of Mother Mary of the Immaculate Conception crushing the serpent. The altar, made of dark wood, is in the center, covered with a white-lace altar cloth. A Bible sits on top of it, lying open – God's sacred Word hearkening. A golden tabernacle sits on a stand against the wall to hold the Holy Eucharist. Stations of the cross are arranged in the chapel throughout: Traditional, simple, and depicting the Passion of Jesus. And that's all. The MCs are like the chapel and their mission – all about the passion of Jesus and equally passionate help for the poor.

Sometimes in life, we can get stuck on the complex and forget the basics, so, keep it simple, as in the Missionaries of Charity's chapel, and in our lives.

Aesthetics. Usually we equate beauty with golden glossiness, movie starlets and glittering outer appearances. Humans, being sensual creatures, look for beauty in the attractive. As the saying goes, beauty, though, is only skin-deep. We usually take and *make* more time for outward, physical preparations, than for inner, metaphysical disciplines. Generally, when people travel, one of the first things they'd want to see are the beautiful sights – palaces, people, trinkets, gardens and dazzlingly-different aspects of God's creations never before witnessed. But we pilgrims are slightly different, extremely expectant when we travel and never want to be bored. We want to see fireworks, not boring vanilla-phenomena! However, it's important to be realistic. We really need to begin to see God in *all* things.

As an aside: While pilgrimaging in India, I remember not worrying or being concerned about my personal appearance, why? This was due to India and her supremely age-old and mesmerizing culture. It's nothing like the preoccupation of cosmetology and egotism of personal pleasure and western selfdom. India really is that different.

Stations of the Cross… in Summer? One day, in the MC's chapel, I was sitting in prayer and heard strange noises. *What was that about?* I didn't know, and it happened another day, too. Then I figured it out. Some sisters walked the chapel, holding a little prayer book or… something – I couldn't tell for certain, as I was supposed to be praying, then realized, they were praying the Stations of the Cross in the dead heat of summer! I was used to praying the Stations only in winter, during Lent. In a way, it was kind of a revelation. Praying the Stations of the Cross, well, it reveals aspects of our faith some of us aren't used to seeing. It recalls to us the historical nature of the suffering Christ. He lived as a real man full of passion who later died a brutal death – killed by other real, historical people.

Reflection is a gateway for thankfulness. In the midst of spirituality, we can sometimes lose, neglect or reject this aspect of history. When we fail to take time for prayer and reflect, we won't be serene within. We actually need helpful objects and memories of prayer, these will help us grow in holiness. Of course, what's difficult these days: Achieving a slower pace, meditating and looking within. Praying the Stations of the Cross – at any time of year – can generate one's need to create an inner life.

Another benefit of praying the Stations? Its devotional quality. Devotions are not emphasized enough today. They are best described as the act of giving one's heart, soul and sentiments to Jesus. Deep stuff, I'd say, and something we shouldn't lose the capacity to do. I learned to reclaim the act of devotion all year around. Each Friday, I try to pray the Stations – lest my spirituality get too unfixed from the sacrificial person of Jesus. I don't want to become forgetful of what He actually did for all of us.

Following this epiphany, I went to a wedding. After the splendor of the ceremony, it was picture-taking time. It became somewhat boisterous. The new couple was certainly off to a great start!

As I was praying in the sanctuary, I noticed an elderly lady, with kids literally running circles around her. She held a little prayer book – reminding me sharply of the MCs in Calcutta – bowed her head, read her prayer book, moved to another Station, bowed her head, read the book, prayed, and moved again. She was totally focused. This is true devotion, something worth keeping, something worth doing, no matter what goes on around you.

HOST WITH THE MOST

Father Bourke was a Canadian Jesuit we'd met on my travels in 1993. The Jesuits were my boon and saving grace – and Father Bourke was one of the grandest. As I traveled from Darjeeling in the north, to Madras in the south – Jesuits were always there: ingratiating, helpful, and a tremendous information resource. If one needs to know local sights and customs of India, ask the Jesuits! As I was a vagrant pilgrim *and* a priest, they fed me and gave me a bunk! Their community spirit was infectious and regenerating; we had meals together, drank beer, had fellowship and played volleyball. They made touring fun. It was in an amazing environment – truly in a home away from home. Jesuits provided welcome and hospitality – the easiest thing to offer, and what's needed the most by travelers in a foreign land!

So, back to Father Bourke. He had hosted our pilgrimage group back in 2005 to Calcutta and Darjeeling. And during our most recent pilgrimage, in 2009, of course, I consulted him again. This man was always smiling, backslapping, and crucially important to us, as he coordinated travel connections and accommodations. Father Bourke could negotiate with beggars in Hindi; he made certain our meals and rooms were prepared. And, he liked hanging around with us, explaining Indian religion, culture and history. And when we wanted to leave Darjeeling a day early, he made this possible – at the last minute! And did all this at age eighty. He'd been serving for fifty years as a priest! That's something wonderful.

One of the biggest and yet subtlest messages I received from Father Bourke? It was his priestly message of commitment to God through serving forever the people of India. He could have gone back to modern, comfortable Canada with friends and family – but chose to *continue* serving God and living out his Spiritual Path in India. This is very much a Jesuit characteristic – follow-through on one's commitment to God. His impressive fortitude showed me how to serve Jesus and His Church, to "keep on keepin' on!" So, no matter your age, you still have an ability to help others. It's important to pace yourself and make practical judgments regarding who you help, and how much. Father Bourke showed me how to extend priesthood throughout my life, and like Melchizedek, be a priest forever.

PURITY

It took a while to realize this, but during my times in India, I didn't see pornography, immodest dress, or reckless sexual behavior. There were none of the sensual challenges usually encountered in magazines, bus advertisements, at beaches or on building facades. Public dress mostly consisted of the ladies' lovely saris, and for men, their attire was generally dignified but not showy. Nor were there public displays of affection – except for parents holding their children's hands. I found it very inspiring, but knew this was not generally the case back home. Not-seeing something of a sensual nature makes it easy to keep a chaste balance in life, but life is *not* like that. One must make a conscious effort to not view (or obsess about) pornography, not expose your conscious mind to overt sensuality in daily life, a true challenge in the west. The lesson I've taken from being in a traditional, old fashioned society? Cleansing one's body-mind-soul cannot be done without personal, daily effort.

EUCHARIST… *Real Presence.*

Every day in India, we pilgrims made a holy hour by doing spiritual reading, sitting in silence, meditating, praying the Rosary, simply hanging out with the Eucharistic Jesus. It takes some effort to plan this, and follow through – especially with our very-full days of work or travel in exhausting heat and oppressive humidity. Weariness was a constant companion. Yet most days, we made holy hour happen; after all, Mother Teresa mandated her sisters to do it (many MCs do two holy hours each day!). I like to call it "Face-time with Jesus". In our busy culture, some may wonder why we Catholics worship Jesus in the Eucharist, a rather static way of honoring Him, one might say. In reality, the Eucharist is actually quite dynamic, we are *in His Presence*, talking and listening to Jesus, and are still with Him as Lord and our Divine Friend. Once you get hooked on doing a holy hour, you can allow it to become a holy habit that will sustain you.

About a year ago, while at a priest-retreat, we were asked to reflect on what sustains us through our priesthood. My answer, Christ in the Eucharist. This holds up through all times, seasons, parishes, changes, friendships, challenges, papacies and bishop-bosses – in essence, the Eucharist persists through all changes (within and without). And I was not the only one who thought so.

In the Eucharist, and in every Mass, Jesus shows that because He loves us so much, He imprints Himself within the Eucharist. Jesus didn't just love us once – He *continues* to love us in and through every Mass, and in every church or chapel we will ever visit! Jesus wants to love us and be remembered to us by nourishing us supernaturally. As an artist puts his or her creative flair into a painting, or a judge makes his mark through the legal system, Jesus extends, and communicates His Real Love and Life into the Eucharist. Think of First Communion, when young girls wear beautiful white dresses and boys sport clumsy new suits. They are getting dressed up for Jesus, so why shouldn't we "dress-up" our souls and lives, as He loves us so lavishly?

My favorite holy hours? For me, it was when we had them at the Motherhouse in Calcutta, where Mother Teresa herself did it twice a day. We looked forward to this, when we'd pray the Rosary before the Blessed Sacrament. People from all over the world would attend, even if they weren't Catholic. After the opening song, the Lord would come upon the altar in the monstrance (unique words that mean "to show"). Next there would be silence. After praying the Rosary, we sat quietly and waited for the benediction, which I, as priest, gave twice, so, no matter how tired, I had to stay awake!

The sisters began singing (in their ethereally-lovely Indian voices); everyone rose from sitting or kneeling and faced the altar for the benediction prayer. There would be total silence and reverence for the benediction – the most sacred part of the liturgy. After prayers and blessings, all would depart the Motherhouse in peace, presumably for home and rest, and to prepare for another day in Calcutta. It was the most appropriate way to close the day. Mother Teresa did it every day of her life – with Jesus the Lord.

I was once assigned to the National Shrine-Grotto in Emmitsburg. It has a beautiful all-glass chapel. During Easter, it was decorated in miles of white ribbon, many golden bows and dozens of lilies. A visitor asked, "Is there a wedding here today?"

I thought: *A wedding... of course,* and said, "Yes. It's Holy Communion."

PRAYER WARRIORS

Once, in Darjeeling, we were running late for early-morning Mass. Some of us were sick, slowing our progress. We walked a long way to the MC convent across town, and saw the magnificent Kanchenjunga Mountain. Naturally, we stopped, gawked, photographed, gawked some more, making us *very* late for Mass. I hurriedly vested, wheezing out frosty breath in the high altitude. I saw one of the MC nuns; she motioned for me to slow down. I took a deep breath, entered the chapel, and was astounded, even embarrassed; there were five nuns kneeling on the floor before the altar and blessed sacrament, praying, wearing big sweaters and blue scarves over their heads, leaning over while meditating, patiently waiting.

They kept vigil, worshiped Jesus and waited in front of Him and His Divine Presence. We were late, and the ladies were cold, but prayerful, being faithful sentinels. They welcomed us after Mass into their courtyard and invited us to breakfast. Of course, we accepted and had a grand time with them, two cats and sick folks living at the convent. The MCs are austere but happy. But the religious reality of those sisters praying in that cold chapel, keeping vigil until we arrived remains within me, inspires me to be vigilant, persevering and loving, like those tenacious nuns!

POOR… AND YET SO RICH

There was a simple man, Francis, a middle-aged Indian who was technically our "servant" at the Church of Seven Dolors. He was always smiling and deferential; ready to help, yet hardly spoke to us. He had a wife and four children. Amidst his many chores, he never looked gloomy.

The concept of servants is obviously a bit difficult for most Americans, but we gradually adapted to this Indian custom. While there was nothing magical about Francis, everyone thought him quite magnificent –probably because he was joyful, always-ready, poor yet cheerful and obviously pragmatic.

One of those ironies of India, while we were in-country to serve the poor with the MCs, others, like Francis, served *us*.

Sacrificial Love. One of the most impressive lessons of India: harsh beauty, as described earlier. The Missionary of Charity sisters give their lives not only to the poorest of the poor, but to each other in religious community. Volunteers work with them, sacrifice to get there and possess the willingness to encounter Jesus in His many guises through the poor walking down the street. We think of love as pleasure, joy and happiness, and it is, but on the other side of the coin, it's a love summarized by Mother Teresa, who said, "Give until it hurts." The main symbol of Christianity is a cross, implying there is a *cost* to love. When I returned from Calcutta from one of my trips, I thought once again, "How will I realize the fruits of this pilgrimage at home?" It's a daunting question that I've heard most pilgrims ask. One answer appeared, practically under my nose…

Her name was Donna. She attended Mass at the National Shrine Grotto, and could have put her radically-disabled autistic son Joseph into a care facility, but never did. He couldn't speak or take care of himself. Donna was his full-time caregiver. Because of her sacrificial love, this single mom brought a now 47-year-old Joseph to daily Mass. He was always on the move and required constant attention. I saw in Donna the face of Calcutta – a daily, radical, ongoing sacrifice of Love –the giving of self to the point of hurt – actually living out the Divine Master's commandment: "Love one another" (Jn. 13:34).

Donna and Joseph lived close by; they did normal and super-normal things not always seen or praised. I have relatives I need to love more. There are other, similar "close-by situations" that can inspire one to holiness. One should "find your own Calcutta," as Mother Teresa used to say. The normal can be an opportunity for finding or creating supernormal manifestation.

One of the best penances – really an ongoing meditation– I ever received was when I went to confession. The priest told me to replace the word 'love" in I Corinthians 13 with my own name and to measure myself against St. Paul's list of loving attributes, I might perfect myself and become more holy, loving and Christ-centered.

Try it, and become converted by actual practice and meditation! We learn by example and illustration. Saintly examples like Joseph and Donna *and* their living of St. Paul's ongoing, incarnational commitment of love shows you how it's done.

> **Meditate upon the famous *"Love Chapter"***
>
> "Love is patient, love is kind. It is not jealous, [love] is not pompous, it is not inflated, it is not rude, it does not seek its own interests, it is not quick-tempered, it does not brood over injury, it does not rejoice over wrongdoing but rejoices with the truth. It bears all things, believes all things, hopes all things, endures all things.Love never fails…" (I Corinthians 13:.4-8)

Sterilization and Burning Candles. One day, we went on a pilgrimage-within-a-pilgrimage, to a shrine near Calcutta. It was a rough trip, after two hours of rutted, terrible roads, we got out of the vehicles, gazed at the tropical setting, then celebrated Mass in a small chapel. The grounds were beautiful, like other Catholic compounds we'd already seen – exotic with flowering trees and plants everywhere.

Then we met a ninety-year-old priest from Italy. Everyone was fascinated, as he was quite charming, youthful in outlook, and seemed to be fascinated with *us*. Living his priesthood in India, we saw and could practically taste his dedication and commitment to Christ. We sang a song and this beautiful priest gave us his benediction. Totally worth the trip, just for that!

Later, when we toured near the statue of Our Lady, I saw a ton of burning candles underneath the likeness. So, I decided to do the pilgrim thing and light a candle. I enjoyed seeing other pilgrims go up, bow and with hands folded, make a prayer to our Lady of Good Voyage. I will always remember that candle-stand, the dripping candles and the devotions. It was a positively incarnational, Catholic and exotic, complete with ornate Indian saris, groups of people, icons, pictures, bells and statuary. I also enjoyed being a pilgrim, taking in the sights, the smells and bells, without worrying about incidentals or clean-up!

Most new American Catholic churches are largely sterile, with hardly any images, candles or devotional spaces, as seen in older churches. In Indian churches, almost everything, even crying, needing and desiring pilgrims, is shared in the open. It was an eye-opening experience.

New-Age and Old Values… Spirituality and Spiritualism. I now live in Hancock, a quaint little town in western Maryland, right on the Potomac River. But, of all things one wouldn't expect, less than ten miles away, in Berkeley Springs, West Virginia is a Tibetan arts and culture center! Years ago, I had to travel thousands of miles, go through China, checkpoints, passport controls, two travel agencies and one visa to reach Tibet. Now, it's virtually next door.

This reminds me how easily one can access Eastern influences today, whether in Berkeley Springs, at a yoga class, or by hanging out with MCs in Calcutta. I saw many westerners at the Motherhouse, trying to soak in some aspect of its lovely spirituality, where Mother Teresa lived her life and did her work. There is a great deal of allure, even today, to be where her spiritual rubber met the road.

More and more people today balk at being associated with institutional religion, seeing it as a block to their "spirituality" (we use this word in quotes since it is so general, personal and intangible). Let's call them "spiritualists". While we Catholics believe in religion *and* spirituality, we may be seen as fossilized faith-dinosaurs. There are plenty of "professional religionists," non-Catholics, usually holy rollers who put on a good show, do a lot of shouting, bring in thousands to their monster churches, moralize a great deal, but fail to mystify.

Here's an even bigger question: What are the reasons contributing to this dire divorce of spirituality and religion? There are multiple causes. See below…

Ritualism. Some spiritual seekers see the Mass as mechanistic and sterile. By contrast, in India, we pilgrims saw and experienced something totally the opposite. Our Masses and spirituality, as one saying goes, demonstrated the *living* tradition of the dead and not the dead tradition of the living. We saw this especially within the Missionaries of Charity. The sisters put their whole hearts into Mass and conduct a deep prayer life – they are souls who genuinely spiritual and very welcoming of others traveling along the Way. Love God, Love Neighbor is what I try to follow as a spiritual program. Nothing dead or sterile about that!

Examples...or lack thereof. Like the Bible professes—"So also faith of itself, if it does not have works, is dead." (Jas. 2:17), so Catholics should connect to both the Mass and the masses. Certainly, this was most true of Mother Teresa. Some are turned off by Catholics, as they may seem to be elitist, snide or not-connected. I remember a couple, Nan and Kirk from New Mexico, who travelled every two years, after saving their money, just to serve in Mother Teresa's homes in Calcutta for several weeks. These are practicing Catholics who love their faith and are setting excellent examples for others to see! Not connected? Elitist? I think not!

Are we Catholics friendly icons, or true windows to Christ? We should be. Many Protestants excel at welcoming others to their communities and faith, we can do it as well and should not leave it up to anyone else!

Moralism. New-Agers are turned off by believers who they perceive as moralistic, that is, embracing commandments, codes and what they perceive as behavioral straitjackets of faith.

And yet, I think of our pilgrims who went to Calcutta specifically to serve the poorest of the poor, and on their own dime! Why? Moralism? No. Because Catholics love loving others!

Catholics have some of the deepest *and* highest spiritual-slash-moral wisdom in the world. We need to share it! After all, our sacred religion produced artists and scientists like Michelangelo, Galileo, Mendel, Pasteur, poets like Gerard Manley Hopkins and Shakespeare; athletes like Vince Lombardi, renaissance men like Leonardo da Vinci and Pope John Paul II. And then there are the greatest of mystics: Saint Teresa of Avila and Saint John of the Cross. For us, religion and spirituality are beautifully inter-woven – NOT moralistic programs to entrap people.

Three Practices for Spirituality
Abandonment repels control.
Selflessness offsets selfishness.
Fasting counters feasting.

Abandonment. It's a form of surrender and letting go – wherein one offsets excessive control of physical and mental realities to learn a new way of living. A severe example of this is what Bible believers recall from Jesus on the Cross, Who cried out: "Father, into your hands I commend My Spirit" (Lk. 23:46), and then died, showing us the Ultimate Surrender, which is really a victory. He thus showed us "Ways to Disappear," wherein we take the next step, and "dissolve ourselves" into selflessness.

Selflessness in Practice. We pilgrims had many opportunities to "disappear", such as when we served the poor. We embraced our simple provisions, underwent sickness and fatigue, learned new and quite foreign ways – and in all these things, we had to "disappear ourselves" from American ways into Indian ways, and in so doing, we found Jesus.

In other words, when we disappear, Jesus will appear more clearly in our lives and work through us. The world emphasizes the direct opposite in advertisements for various things, such as: "Be all you can be", "I am somebody." Although there are certain truths to some of these statements, as Christians, it's actually a matter of letting go of *excessive control,* because, after all, we do need some direction over some things, but not too much or we'll become headstrong, egotistic and addicted to manipulation.

We need to abandon *idealistic abandonment* as an enemy, that is, the dream that all things will be easy after one achieves enlightenment and one can therefore make a simple slide into life's lessons without any decisions, ego or reasoning –going on automatic pilot without need of conscious reflection. This is the danger of some Eastern spiritualities. After learning more of life's lessons, and, of course, God's lesson, I realized it is a balance of *letting go* and *going forth* in the right ways, and the right times and to the right places!

Heed this from the famed Latin maxim: *In media stat virtu / In the middle, lies virtue*. It's not either-or, not being totally controlled or becoming a jovial joker. The answer is, rather *both/and*—utilizing some control and at other times, surrendering to allow the flow of situations and other persons to guide you. It is sometimes easier to go to one extreme or another– total freedom or absolute control. HOWEVER, one results in existentialism, the other in fascism. It is, admittedly, more difficult to make a "middle approach" work, but worth it.

Jesus said, "Deny yourself" (Lk. 9:23). An example? One pilgrim spontaneously paid for another pilgrim's taxi ride; our tour director bought all twelve of us a meal. When one pilgrim got sick in a Darjeeling restaurant, another offered to walk him home.

Fasting and feasting. In India, the food was sometimes wildly spicy, and hard to eat, but if you're really hungry, you'll give it a go and hope for the best. Then there was the feast-or-famine syndrome. At times, someone spoiled us with a home-cooked meal, and then at other times, we quite literally did not where our next meal might come from, or if we would eat at all—that happened more than once! Then it became a kind of involuntary fasting, a "reactive asceticism" to offset gluttony and, more positively, to develop practice in self-mastery. If we hadn't gone to India, we might not have gained this type of wisdom. It was something to think about, once back home. Self-mastery – that is, to *not* indulge – takes practice!

SERVING SPIRITUALITY

"Whoever does not love a brother whom he has seen cannot love God– Who he has not seen…" (I Jn. 4:20)

Probably the most spiritual thing our pilgrims did in India – besides shared Masses and holy hours – was to serve others. I not only heard daily our pilgrims' godly glee, but saw it on their faces. *That* was what they wanted to do the most, serve! Whether associating with poor clients in Darjeeling's social centers or at Prem Dan in Calcutta, our pilgrims thoroughly enjoyed religious outreach. Sometimes service meant bathing men and women. Humbling? Yes, it was, and fulfilling, too. For each person doing this, combined with God's mysterious Designs, each brought his or her unique personal alchemy of holiness to these places.

I was inspired just how spiritual all this was for our pilgrims, especially after struggling to get there, surviving very-hot cuisine, early morning wake-up calls, long walks and bus rides just to serve. Many thought their pilgrimage was the best thing they had ever experienced.

Sometimes in our lives, we try to dodge some of these "bullets" – serving, getting messy, undergoing hardship and challenges, making a sacrifice –these are all barriers to genuine spirituality. But that's what Christians are about – a holy way of life by maximizing love of God and loving our neighbor. It's the vertical and horizontal need to somehow become fused.

Catherine of Siena, Pope John Paul II, Mother Teresa, there are so many excellent examples of holy people who loved God and neighbor with great zeal and yet had balance.

Holiness is a term that needs to come back into daily use!

As a spiritual pilgrim on the road to Heaven, I take delight in serving others, and not just because I'm a priest. When I serve others, I learn much from them. Others enjoy novenas and rosaries and still others employ realization of one's selfhood.

So, why do this?

The Missionaries of Charity spirituality is incarnational, very much giving and doing in-the-flesh – not a theology class, head-trip or idealistic self-actualization. The MCs live that great balance between love of God and love of neighbor, literally going into the gutters of sludge, as their spirits soar into the heavens. They find the Face of Christ in the Eucharist and in the poor they serve. They show humility before God and their fellow man. They love the chapel and the neighborhood.

INTERLUDE - PART 1

HOW DO YOU LOVE YOUR NEIGHBOR?

> "Actions speak louder than words. Let your
> words teach and your actions speak."
> —St. Anthony of Padua

Love… MC-Style

Love God. At daily Mass, usually at six in the morning, Mother Teresa would kneel on the bare floor and manifest a love relationship with Jesus Christ in the Eucharist. Yes, she really did.

So, how do *you* show your love to God? Are you able to go to daily Mass or, at least, Mass once a week other than Sunday? Are you reading the Bible regularly? Are you receiving God's graces through prayer and deeper prayer in mediation?

Love Neighbor. Mother Teresa used to quote Jesus in the Last Judgment (Mt. 25:40) when He refers to people who did corporal works of mercy: "You-did-it-to-Me" – and He meant that literally. We did those kindnesses to *Him* the Lord. Mother Teresa became an eloquent respected "preacher-teacher" precisely because she walked the talk and consistently lived the Gospel. Everyone saw that.

Do you serve others?

Visualize a bulls-eye target in regard to charitable works…

The outermost ring is what's largest and represents your family, the easiest to serve (usually!).

The next inner ring represents serving your friends, and it's relatively easy to serve them, too. The last ring – the center – is the smallest and hardest to embrace.

The bulls-eye stands for the poor, sick and dying, those who are different and sometimes challenging, not in your comfort zone and consist of people who might not ever thank you.

Our vocation? We travel through the various "rings" and deal with the challenges within them. In essence, we "disappear" ourselves and heroically serve, like the saints, by loving others and God first.

First things first. While Mother Teresa valiantly served others – the poorest of the poor, there was never a doubt in my mind of her First Love – God. She balanced love of God and neighbor, for sure, as few others have shown us in our lifetime. However, the first thing in the morning and last thing at night was prayer and adoration. She spent ample time by loving God in the sacraments and meditation. Not everything is equal in the spiritual life – we must make God first and everything else will follow – even the seemingly all-important and imminent things which will not wait.

MOTHER TERESA'S DARKNESS

Have you read or seen Mother Teresa's book *Come Be My Light*? This book revealed another side of Mother Teresa, unknown to most: her struggles with dryness in prayer and the darkness of her interior life, trials of understanding God and the seeming absences of Him. Although many Christians experience this in their lives, Mother Teresa underwent decades of it. But she still went on, believed and served amidst these troubles. This phenomenon is otherwise known as the "dark night of the soul". It is not unusual and, in fact, is an inevitable facet of the spiritual life for some, and for many, becomes a celebrated major pathway to God.

A mystical writer once wrote: "The spiritual life is not one of addition but of subtraction." This makes a good point that flies in the face of our western analytical heritage –we always try to figure things out and find an explanation for everything. The tendency of some

New-Age philosophies to accept only a sunny-sided view of things, well, obviously, divine darkness doesn't fit in there very well.

Western Catholics and Christians have another difficulty—we sometimes fail in honoring mystery. What does that mean? Mostly because western culture is rife with excessive rationality and positivism. These are huge influences, and makes it challenging to accept God as Mystery, as something beyond us. Yes, accepting limitations of the intellect, the suffering nature of souls and dark alchemy of salvation goes against those possessed of analytical minds. In the Christian East, there is a much more positive emphasis upon the Mystery of God and His Hidden-ness –all in good ways, which reveal man's stature, showing us as small before the Lord, Who is tall.

Mother Teresa was in that darkness of soul, but didn't become part of it, nor did she let it overcome her. Only at the end of her life, did she document these things. When assessing her dark relationship, some think then she was not authentic – that she lacked in her personal relationship with Christ. Others (atheists and skeptics, of course) think she was a scam. But still others are thankful for her revelation and struggle with darkness, that she could admit to it, but also for the revelation, revealing that a saint is, after all, really just like us – a human being filled with ambiguities and challenges – and further reveals that the God of mystery and majesty we worship doesn't just automatically fit into clean categories – He doesn't just appear and reveal Himself fully because a person has become holy. Mother Teresa's story is a testimony to human perseverance in the face of difficulty and God's grace. God helps us persist; He gives us strength to "keep on keepin' on!" This sainted lady continues to inspires people like me to seek the Kingdom and the Lord and to always persevere.

PRIESTLY ZEAL

Contrasting with the darkness referred above, there is a person of tremendous talent and creativity you need to know about, Father Sunil Rosario. He had a fine connection to the Missionaries of Charity, and was a man always on the move – physically and mentally – constantly conjuring up some plan for his parish, his diocese, or even for us while visiting!

History. Father Sunil visited Orissa State (just southwest of Calcutta, now called Odisha) to minister to persecuted Christians and Missionaries of Charity there. He met a man who'd been seriously attacked by some Hindus, and it made him renounce Christ. But, after speaking extensively with Father Sunil, the man re-professed his faith in Christ – essentially, Father Sunil had been able to calm down the man, so that they could pray the Our Father together. It was that re-commitment of faith, inspired by Father Sunil's wisdom and ability to be a Good Shepherd that was so exciting and meaningful to me. I'm not sure how I would have reacted in a similar situation.

I then thought: *How many people would go out and document such suffering?* Father Sunil's beautiful and living faith gave him the ability to go forward, and retain the tenacity to travel and spread the Word of Christ.

INTERLUDE - PART 2

"Praise and bless my Lord, and give him thanks
and serve him with great humility."
—St. Francis of Assisi

A PILGRIMAGE-*TO*-SERVE

Effects and Counter-Effects

As pilgrims, we obviously didn't go to India on a whim; we were all religiously influenced in some way, each with his or her own spirituality, goals and desires. In today's internet-mass-media, commercialized-globalized world, there are tons of influences upon Christians today, including missionary work.

SO...WHAT INFLUENCED US?

Psychology. Part of the spiritual battle in going on pilgrimage to India is to not give in to stereotypes and intimidation – the heat, masses of people, gigantic poverty, beggars, bad water, and spicy food. Meanwhile, we have seen how psychology has inspired religion in a positive way through genuine inner development – and negatively, by excessive self-actualization to the detriment of God's role, others and service. This latter path can become happiness at any cost. As with many things, a healthy balance of psychology and religion is needed. Our pilgrims overcame busy travel schedules, challenging service opportunities, extreme fatigue, foreign foods and languages, individual mind-states and moods. So, it's a good idea to avoid the extremes – especially ignorance and self-preoccupation – and realize what St. Irenaus said, "The Glory of God is man fully alive."

Sociology. I am sure many of our youth on pilgrimage were positively influenced by sociology's message of "global village" and "help your neighbor" and "We're all of the same DNA" and so forth. Sociology has positively influenced spirituality, to integrate social justice into spiritual teachings and yet, there needs to be a warning attached, in that sociology doesn't negatively boil down religion to a set of humanistic, patterned customs and shared values. Globalism has affected religious folk extremely well, and shows us that our "neighbor" is all over the world. Sociology can definitely influence youth and others today through volunteerism and good multi-culturalism. Our pilgrims enjoyed meeting foreigners in a dizzyingly-different culture and rose to the sociology occasion.

Philosophy. Are we more "one" than we think? That's India's thought and contribution. Pilgrims on our trip at some level sought this, finding that oneness incarnate by hanging out together, helping others to Mass and praying through the intercession of the saints.

Philosophy asks questions like: What is life? Is there a God? What is my responsibility in the world? These are healthy and essential investigations into life and yet, answers can become exaggerated, as seen in existentialism (I am the center of any meaning in life), individualism (there is no absolute or law outside me), monism (all is one). We pilgrims learned that Indian people we met were not "philosophers on the street" eschewing ideological mantras but, rather, real humans desiring interaction, love and respect. We met them where they were amidst larger philosophical queries that faded into the quiet as we addressed real concerns with folks who wanted and needed help.

We found many explorations into the local cultures of India fascinating, and at times thrilling. Our pilgrims were – and hopefully still are – seekers of Truth. While having found that Truth – incarnate in Jesus Christ – we still search for, and uncover new expressions of, that truth. Truth is all around us, and India is a marvelous place to make that discovery! Many of the young pilgrims were raised in rather traditional church families with strong religious identity, however, they discovered wonder and joy in India, learning something new each day.

"But seek first the kingdom [of God] and his righteousness, and all these things will be given you besides" (Mt, 6.33).

All these influences recounted obviously had varied effects upon us. In essence, for Catholics and Christians, it boiled down to Love God, Love Neighbor. Translated: re-living the Life of Jesus Christ, each in our own unique way, sometimes by establishing some kind of pattern, as recounted below…

A TYPICAL DAY

Was there one? Of course not. But here *was* our "Indian routine":

0600: Wake up, and then attempt to corral several really-sleepy-sluggish pilgrims into a huddle. It's kind of like trying to collect a thousand feathers shaken from a pillowcase, or herding cats. Get one sleepy-head out of bed, another and another, then the first one has already disappeared into sleep, challenging eh?!…

0615: Now, this is early for most travelers, err, pilgrims on "vacation". We begin the walk to the Motherhouse for Mass. It's dark and we're already tired. We have to move quickly, we're late, as usual. Hardly anyone talks. Most are zombie-like, part-human, forming a train of walkers down the street. Nothing straightforward about this walk, however: We have to dodge beggars, even this early, and vendors, the inevitable buses and swerving taxis. And you can't step on the bodies sleeping on the sidewalks/pavements – yes, sometimes whole families! For me, this was quite surreal, and probably one of the most eye-opening experiences for any of us. It's one thing to help homeless people in a shelter or a soup kitchen, but quite stunningly another to see and *step over them* in their literal on-the-street homelessness.

0650-ish: We arrive at the Motherhouse, go through the parlor, enter a courtyard, take off our shoes and put them in a pile with dozens of others – and hope you get the same shoes back! There are predominantly flip-flops and sandals, but regular shoes, too. You feel a little self-conscious taking off a prized possession – what literally separates you from the streets of Calcutta.

Then it's up a polished stairway, and at the first landing there's a large, life-size crucifix on the wall with a definitely delirious-looking divine Jesus on it: very MC-ish: gnarly; the earthy-gritty Divine Christ has eyes half-sad and half-anguished. Nearby on the pallid wall is an expansive world map with little colored pins on it – indicating where all MC missions have been established – and trust me, they are all over the world. Alongside this was a little chalkboard with an inspirational-quote of Mother Teresa written in bright chalk. The Chapel is right next to this stairwell and awaits us.

0700 Mass. This was *the* highlight of the day. Once inside the chapel, you found a place on the floor amidst so many other pilgrims – dozens of volunteers on one side of the chapel, a hundred MC sisters in the middle and on the far side. All is quiet when we arrive. Then the priestly procession starts from the outer hallway-balcony. The MCs would sing, in English, as Calcutta woke up outside the chapel.

After Mass was breakfast, the simplest of meals – what we would call a continental breakfast–biscuits (sometimes lightly sweet) and tea with lots of milk and brown sugar if you wanted it. Then, before leaving, we'd sing a ministry song, usually with a big yelp at the end.

After breakfast we'd walk to our ministry site, which, for us, was at Prem Dan. This usually took twenty minutes *if* we followed the right way down the proper alleys. One time we got *really* lost. After asking directions from several people, it was suggested to me that we take taxis; eventually I acquiesced, got us out of that laborious labyrinth – a harrowing and nerve-racking experience.

Morning work. Prem Dan is a living center for men and women. For men-pilgrim-volunteers, our job was to do the wash – a Big Job. You immediately put on an apron, and did laundry for one hundred and fifty residents. The guys lined up at a long trough with many basins, wash tubs and faucets, and started working, hopefully at a picked duty, but if you arrived late, you filled in, doing whatever was needed. Lady pilgrims went to an upper floor, visited with the women-clients, and gave them light breakfasts.

We then cleaned up our work areas and scrubbed the interior of Prem Dan – walkways and plazas in a very-large courtyard. Just so you know, our compound was surrounded by thick, high walls. Cleaning water came from underground spigots. We filled buckets and carried them everywhere, then used primitive whisk brooms to first swish the water on the pavement, then sweep away dirt and trash. This was physically demanding. By the time the job was done, we were sweating, even it wasn't yet very hot. Time for a rest.

1100: Morning break. Some of us would socialize with other volunteers and learn about their "journey" to Calcutta and, of course, it was important to drink *chai*, tea, or water (definitely due to the exertion), and biscuits, more like wafers – a delight even though simple. There was a pavilion for us to rest out of the sun, near green plants. Some of my favorite times was spent sitting on that veranda, catching my breath and talking to people.

Late morning. Our task was now to get the men ready for lunch – their main meal of the day –and had to have everything ready by noon. We got out silver-metal bowls and cups; we didn't need utensils as everyone ate Indian style – with the hands. About a third of the men needed to be lifted from their beds, and helped to sit. Only a few stayed in bed; most others, we directed to a line, where they sat or squatted to eat. The meal was usually some kind of rice and dal (a mixture of vegetables and sauce). Sometimes there was chicken, beef or fish. The men were usually eager to eat and very expectant. A gigantic bowl of rice was brought out; the virginal rice always looked so beautiful – pristine white and steaming. Then a large basin of the *dal* and vegetables came next. One of the volunteers or sometimes a Missionary of Charity would ladle food elements into each dish.

Then the men who could walk came to the table of food first; volunteers helped serve. Other volunteers took food to the men who couldn't walk, out to the courtyard. It was an efficient and very-human MC process. Not quiet, mind you. There was lots of clanging, sometimes yelling and demands, and the usual calls for more food. Most of the men would simply accept their lot of food without emotion, I noticed, kind of in a daze.

Clean-up. After lunch, of course, it was time to wash plates and cups, not to mention scrubbing down the courtyard. Then it was time for washing of a different sort, bathing people. For the men, this might also involve shaving, getting a back-rub, or other muscle-massage. This was a new thing for me, and quite a steep learning curve, especially as my 'clients' spoke no English, and/or were sometimes mentally handicapped. Massages were harrowing, as I never knew just how much pressure to apply, who was wounded and who wasn't. Facial expressions helped with some of that.

Afternoon. We left Prem Dan after noon clean-up, right out of the calm and dignity of the MC's compound into the nightmare of Calcutta's slums. Little children played –and preyed – upon the unsuspecting, defecated nearby, then begged us for food. Once we successfully got through this nightmare, we walked along a high terrace above the compound to taxi stands and bus stops – once again experiencing the thrill of another Indian people-morass. Generally, we'd have lunch back at Our Lady's Church. Some of our youth would play soccer in the church compound; some went shopping, strolled down the street and killed time, and still others took a siesta. For me, just getting back after our morning labors was a singular victory. During winter months in India, noon to 5:00 p.m. was the hottest time of day.

Evening. Sometimes we'd go on a tour with Father Sunil, visit a convent or have a festive dinner – allwere enjoyable and brought our group together, along with meeting local Indians. Other times, we would go to holy hour at around seven at the MC Motherhouse, usually walking over, very carefully, I might add.

Occasionally, we'd go shopping in the evening at a Calcutta bazaar (really a mall) to buy gifts and negotiate with vendors – sometimes that got a little exciting. We then took two taxis… yes, each crammed with six of us, and, in a kind of race, made it to the MC Motherhouse just in time for worship! I really enjoyed seeing all those people…even if they were there for reasons other than worship. It was always an inspiration and a good witness for our young pilgrims.

> Dinner in India was always interesting. Like Europeans, we ate late – usually at around eight. By that time, one of two things happened: Either people ate a lot or they ate hardly anything. Sometimes the food was so unique, spicy or unusual and, combined with folks being so tired, they might manage a few bites and kind-of collapse on the table, waiting for everyone else to finish. Meals were sumptuous, with appetizer, entreé and dessert.

Night-Bedtime. Usually we were exhausted by evening, some of our days meant arriving at our lodging just in time for bed. We were ready to collapse! Given so much action during the day, new experiences and learning so much, it was lot to process. And knowing we'd be up again at 0600 to do it all over again, we slept the sleep of the just, at least I did, most nights, unless those dogs would start barking. Grr…

LESSONS LEARNED

It's humbling to receive service and charity from others – especially when you're in India, one of the poorest places in the world and *we* are the ones getting treated and spoiled. The very reason we pilgrims went over was to serve *others*. That's why it's called a service trip, duh. It's also called a "pilgrimage," precisely because you don't always know what you're getting into, or where God will appear that day. Often when we received a meal or gift from a host, our knee-jerk reaction within would be: *I didn't come for this—I came to serve!*

So, after going through various mental tugs-of-war within ourselves – as if trying not to lose our focus, we pilgrims did learn to see *and accept* charity as godly blessings. Like, when a kid on the street gave us a taste of his drink or outcasts smiled at us… yes, those are truly blessings in a place like India. This "curveball" – graciously receiving rather than giving – it made us *paradoxical pilgrims*, as we went for one thing and got another. We thought we were servants and discovered we would be served – and that this was just as humbling. We received gifts from poor people, and it just as much a gift for us to wash their dishes or give them food. We learned that Catholic pilgrims could do the Catholic *both / and* thing: serve others *and* receive their service to us. We went to India to grow, think and thank; we were sent forth to bring others the Good News, and received that same Good News ourselves.

Open to God's unfolding gifts

We memorized this saying abovie, five important words for the five fingers of one hand. What do they mean?

Open: As a dynamic mental state implies, we need to release control, and not be chained by so many things or ideas, nor should we be or oppressed by past baggage. And, *open* also means to be expectant and actively desirous of what God is going to give us in His time and His way. Open implies to activate yourself and to *be* open – wait for the epiphany to appear.

to God's: God above is the giver of all good things, the Source of salvation, our healing and our wholeness. "God is love" (I Jn. 4:8), and He gave us His only Son as redemption. They say He created the world simply by "being Himself" – as in Love overflowing and making the world. In this sense, it's a continuous unfolding of – in our case as pilgrims – Indian smells, sights and sounds (people greeting us), the many lunches and dinners we received as gifts. We experienced God in the Indian people, and through the language and joy of the poor. God is the giver and we receive His very gifts.

Unfolding: It means the spontaneous manifestation of the mosaic of God's infinite Divinity cascading into humanity and creation. It also implies the blessings that come from Him that are right in front of our eyes and under our noses. Like when we were treated to a tour of Calcutta in shiny new Land Cruisers –spacious, high off the ground, clean and fast – right after getting out of jammed taxis which polluted us to near-exhaustion. We hungry humans need to stop looking for the magical rainbow "way over there" and see God's gifts unfolding within our space and time – wherever we are.

Unfolding can be a curveball of revelation, sometimes. In our case, this meant seeing and then accepting (at some level) the difficulty that our returning-home-plane had been grounded by smog. *There's a blessing in this somewhere!* I recall reading once about a priest who was a victim of a car accident, and put on bed-rest – not even able to say Mass – for weeks and learned this was God's "gift" to him – not one he would have chosen. But it was the way this restriction forged that priest into a greater solidarity of likeness with Christ-as-Victim.

Each day for us pilgrims was a revelation of God's love for us – not always pretty – there were surprises and at other times, we were shell-shocked.

Open to God's unfolding gifts. Bottom line: They are GIFTS – sometimes unmerited treats or overt surprises which delight and enthrall. A gift in religion is unmerited grace freely given by God or, by someone corporeal. Sometimes, on pilgrimage you're looking for Really Big Things. But hopefully, we've trained ourselves to see everything as a gift, something given-bestowed-unfolded by the Gift-Giver. Examples: Free smiles. Once, while out and about, an Indian school group appeared out of nowhere and in their strikingly-colorful uniforms took a photo with us in the courtyard of their school. Another time, we shared delicious Christmas treats and tea with Mother Teresa's original sisters in a Calcutta convent after singing Christmas songs. If you see something as a grace and freely bestowed from above, it doesn't matter what or who it is, simply that it *is,* and that you are receptively grateful for it. The trick is to be like the dying priest at the end of Bernanos' *Diary of a Country Priest*, who said: *"tout l'grace"* – all is grace: *everything* is a gift.

One of our struggles on pilgrimage: Comparing our lives in the present roughshod moment of India to back-home comforts, and again remembering: *This isn't Club Med*. We exerted more effort to see God's grace through it all.

Maybe you've heard the phrase, *God writes straight with crooked lines*. We've all interpreted life and God's Ways as something like that. Our goal in life is *spiritual integration,* which means we may not always understand *how* God is working in our lives, but we trust that He *is* working through mysterious means. Translation: We saw sometimes-gruesome suffering and super-surprises, we can't totally fathom God's ways. Being open to anything God sends our way can be our teacher and guide in life, going toward Eternal Life!

LIFE IS LIKE THAT

I once visited a priest friend who had been recently diagnosed with cancer, and he told me: "I accept all this as part of God's plan, sending me this, or allowing it. It's all a gift and I thank Him."

Wowa! I was stunned, with that deer-in-the-headlights look. As I knew him and his faith-life well, it was in his character, but still, you don't hear that everyday. His suffering and, more importantly, his reaction to that suffering made his Faith into something beautiful, a profound demonstration of love and surrender.

It's the "Romans-8 Principle" as a living sermon. "All things work together for those who love God…" (Rm. 8:28). The sacred Bible text doesn't say *some* things or *spiritual experiences*" or *joyful* things that would work for our salvation, but ALL things. St. Paul rather said that "*all* things work together" and adds," for those who love God".St. Paul ought to know about suffering, as he was imprisoned and a rejected apostle – he went through it all and allowed it *in Christ* to become material for transformation into Christ-likeness.

So frequently, we saw many poor people in India, but they weren't despairing or sulking, after all, they don't have that choice. At some level, they accepted their present situation and made the best of it. We saw many nuns who had great challenges, big tasks and "kept on keepin' on". Mother Teresa got tossed a lot of curveballs in her life, but she kept progressing. She moved far away from her comfort zone in Europe where she grew up, travelled to India as a religious sister, and willingly adopted a radically new way of life. She rolled with the punches. So, next time you think you're stuck in a difficult situation, it might be part of a mystical encounter with Jesus.

What you learn and go through in life is part of that Journey to God. All becomes part of His salvation for you. Sometimes we think: *This does not belong to my religious story…That is not spiritual*, or, *I can't embrace this!* We shouldn't separate any anything from Salvation's Path. Part of the spiritual journey *is* journeying, making new paths, actually walking upon them before spiritual "completion," going through surprises, trials and tribulations, *integrating all parts of life* into God's mysterious alchemy of salvation.

Fr. Bede Griffith's grave in Tamil Nadu, Shantivanaam, South India

Learn the lesson of integrating surprises. Well, at least we tried, even when someone got lost, felt sick, when we waited (and waited) for tickets, hoping our flight wouldn't be cancelled. Every day on our pilgrimage, someone got sick – always somebody different, whether from the cold (in Darjeeling), pollution (in Calcutta), spicy food (everywhere), air travel or sheer exhaustion. For many, this *was* the pilgrimage. That always prompted another change in the schedule for our "sick person of the day". Sometimes these changes weren't easy, but we stuck together as a team, regardless of circumstances. Darjeeling gave us the most problems: five of us had head colds, high temperatures and drowsiness…some had altitude sickness, plus gastrointestinal issues. Since our lodgings weren't heated, all twelve us jammed into one room trying to stay warm. A major detour in our pilgrimage, to be sure, and meant we had to leave Darjeeling sooner than planned, my call. While it felt like a defeat for me, at first, I must admit to later feeling great relief, in seventy-degree heat, dry conditions and sunshine, heavenly balm and welcome Spring – release and reward!

And before you ask, no, I did NOT get sick. Thankfully, I'm "three for three", in my trips to India. The only trouble was that pulled muscle in my right calf and subsequent ankle-swelling, all due to my rather silly accident in 2009 running barefoot, already discussed.

What I admired in those who did get sick was their bounce-back-ability. Not so sure I'd have done so well. They taught me by their example and fortitude, they kept on keepin' on; sickness was a temporary setback. Worst case scenario? One guy got sick in our hotel, right after hearing our flight home had been cancelled. Food poisoning, we thought…he looked deathly sick – in bed, under covers, getting sicker; he could barely move. We almost called for a doctor. Amazingly, after learning our flight had been rescheduled for later that night, he got better, or at least well enough to move! Noble suffering? Maybe so. But knowing he was about to fly home might have been a great motivator!

CHAPTER 3

Mother Teresa, who said, *We should give of ourselves, even when it becomes hurtful*, is an inspiration to us all.

It's All Part of The Pilgrimage

One of the common knee-jerk reactions in western life – especially in America – is to repel difficult situations. One of the Big Things learned in India on my 2009 Pilgrimage: We Americans protect ourselves from many tough experiences and hardships, assuming one has enough money and talent, anyway, we sure make a good run at it!

This truth comes to me because of the contrast experience – living in the first world one day and the next day living in a third-world country. One moment you have a modern washing machine, and the next you're doing hand-laundry in a sink. One day you're cooking on your big stove, and the next you're doing Ramen noodles on a makeshift hot-plate in your bedroom. One moment you're taking vitamins and prescription meds, and the next you trying to find a simple aspirin. One day you're living in a large house with carpeting and a microwave, and the next you're chasing crickets out of your Indian apartment before taking a shower. Most Americans prefer comforts, to somehow get around difficulties, and make things easier. But as pilgrims, those comforts may not exist, you have to somehow "make do".

"BISCUITS and TEA TOUR"

Through our pilgrimage, we were kinda' "hijacked", as our hosts had various agendas for us that we didn't know about or couldn't foresee. So, while being "hijacked," we became "inculturated", and ate a lot of food along the way. Part of our goal on pilgrimage was to expose ourselves to as many different venues and populations and outreach-service centers as possible, and this sometimes meant we were at the whim of others. While we wanted to do as much service as possible, it seemed rather we were frequently eating and drinking a lot – which, in India, wasn't exactly a bad thing. We eventually learned it is a custom in India to host visitors with biscuits and tea, especially in the afternoon (a holdover from the British Raj—tea time still reigns!) So, we drank lots of tea and ate many biscuits in many places – often unexpectedly. This became a subject of discussion amongst our pilgrims who expected to do mission activities rather than "endure High Tea eats and treats". Some of the pilgrims gave this aspect a moniker (without my knowledge): "biscuits and tea tour," describing our activities during those days, although I didn't know this description at the time. I also knew something needed adjusting in our schedule.

I talked to Father Sunil; he eventually got our drift that we wanted to be more serving than being served, however, his kindly intention of exposing us to a lot of different venues and hospitality was relaxing and enjoyable – we just did it less. Sometimes you need to tell someone your feelings and expectations and expect both the worst and the best.

Amidst all these visits – our hosts were mostly religious sisters in convents, but some lay people and others in nursing homes and elsewhere – we graciously received their hospitality and friendliness, even if we had other plans at those times, and eventually learned to like this way of pilgrimaging. You could call it "adapting to a curveball," these were certainly easier than getting sick or missing a flight!

WATCH OUT WHAT YOU PRAY FOR

On my first night in India, I survived India's barking dogs, mostly because I was massively jet-lagged, we had arrived in Calcutta at three that morning; there wasn't much night left after we hit the sack at four. Believe it or not, before arrival at our lodging, we took a walk through an indoor market. Amazing was the volume of produce, at that hour! But on the second night, sleep was impossible. There were two guard dogs in our church courtyard. Their barking was loud, vicious, and constant. It went in stages: three minutes of rowdy barking and then two minutes of silence, then the enraged barking began again, and then silence. This went on for about two hours. What made it worse, was a courtyard. The barking echoed everywhere, and my room was right above it. I thought: *What's gonna give – the dogs or me? Either they'll stop barking on their own, or I will simply accept it... passively. After all, this is India – the place of transcendence, right?* I tried to ignore the barking, thinking someone would solve the problem, but it continued. I finally got out of bed and tried to find help – a guard or watchman to wrangle the dogs, but there was no one. I resorted to yelling for help, again, nothing.

Somehow, I did get a little sleep toward the later morning – the dogs must have been put away before dawn, as the courtyard opened up when the local school day started. Later that day, I eagerly told some fellow pilgrims about it, hoping they would have some helpful clues to solve the problem or at least share in my upset, especially since the majority of them were sleeping right near the dogs at the courtyard level. I was surprised. They acted as if the dogs weren't a bother, or at least like it wasn't as much of a problem. Needless to say, I felt worse, like I wasn't accepting a trial and growing from it. Then someone said *"It's all part of the pilgrimage!"*

Yikes. Nothing like getting my own words thrown back at me. I took it stride, and didn't complain about the dogs again.

FINDING GOD IN ALL THINGS

Poorest section of the poor in Calcuta with MC sisters and bodyguard

While riding in a taxi through Calcutta, I had a *theophany* (which means literally from the Greek: *God-appearance*). We were nervously trying to get to the Missionary of Charity Motherhouse one night for Rosary and Benediction. I was to be the celebrant – and of course, we were running late after spending time on a shopping spree. We finally hailed a taxi and had to go through winding streets, alleys, mostly, cluttered with shoppers, vendors, animals, tents filled with auto tools and fabrics. It wasn't a long drive –twelve minutes, but it seemed longer.

On the way, I observed our driver. He obviously looked ready for the challenge we'd presented him, knew we were desperate, and rose to the occasion. During that hair-raising ride (when I wasn't looking left and right, expecting accidents) I'd glance at him. He had what I'd call a "charming grimace." There was fire in his eyes and eagerness to his demeanor, *Ahh,* I told myself, *this is God manifesting Himself!* God showed me another side of His Love and Being, albeit in an unusual way. Saint Ignatius one said in a maxim, that one should be "*finding God in all things.*" Well, that day, I most certainly did! We made it to the Motherhouse – and on time, too! Use every event as God's Providence unfolding to reveal Himself to us!

PATIENCE – LEARNING FROM THE BLIND

While working at Prem Dan, I saw a blind man leading fellow pilgrim Paul, as they walked around the courtyard. While everyone else was busy doing laundry, scrubbing walkways, feeding clients, these two guys were holding hands and just, walking. Paul was being led by a blind man! That was his task for that moment in time, a great contrast to his other life – busy, in-demand being productive and multi-tasking, but not in India, not that day. He looked so serene, so mild, trying to communicate in a blend of English and Hindi, and never stopped smiling for that entire hour.

It was a lesson in simplicity and surrender, to not always give in to complex multi-tasking, if it isn't required. Realize that sometimes, we're meant to simply accompany another person –walk with someone, be in solidarity with that person. be in the moment. I'd walked with him earlier for only a few minutes, but I wasn't peaceful. Paul was in his element, however. God showed the face of dedication and patience. Later, the blind guy said to Paul, "I'm checking on your work." Hmm. *His words,* or *God's?* Food for thought.

Reactive Theology. There were instances on our pilgrimage that we experienced some type of mental, physical or financial curveball and had to react. Hinduism stresses the "eternal recurrence of the same" –as does Buddhism and most eastern religions. Translation: Same old, same old. Remember the story in Greek mythology of Sisyphus rolling his rock up a hill, again and again? God looked at the world at around year-Zero B.C., saw that things weren't getting any better and sent His only Son Jesus to be Savior of the World. God saw what needed to be done and responded. The response to 'same old, same old' in Christianity points to God, Who decided to settle things through His Son Jesus. Part of the Pilgrimage of Life, then, is that we should receive Jesus into our hearts in great affection, and we should also make Him our life-changer.

Physical challenges. We walked, and walked, a lot, whether going to and from work, and being constantly on our feet during work. So, when I hurt my foot being careless, that was more than a bummer, it inconvenienced a lot of people. Other people's illnesses added more challenges. We helped each other, used our skills, and compassion, knowing that the sooner folks got well, the rest of us would, too, especially in morale!

Mental challenges. We were always tired; fatigue was a constant companion, and made day-to-day planning difficult, the daily barrage of extreme poverty everywhere, bad smells, they added to one's internal daily debate, *Why am I here? Remind me again, God.* And He would. Most times, our responses were helpful, healthy, up-building. We didn't give in to hysteria, being over-reactive and were never denigrating, well, most of the time. God helped us keep our responses healing and refreshing.

Religion itself is a response, a reverential reaction to life, or lack thereof. The word religion means "to bind together". So, things on earth are askew and separate; the goal of religion is oneness, unity and healing. God heals us. Even in the midst of poverty and injustice, we saw so much joy and happiness. If people in the Black Hole of Calcutta are happy, why can't I be? If they're doing so much with so little, then how can I live a simpler life? God gives us the gift of intellect, and the ability to remember, not to fawn over the past, but to learn from it.

Food challenges. Some Americans, when travelling, want to eat something familiar in a foreign country. We American-Indian pilgrims were no different, and looked for the "usual suspects" – steak, pizza, fries, pasta and even beer! Actually, we rarely found them, and ate what we could find, and acted like it was good, even if it wasn't. Sometimes we couldn't tell what it was, vegetables mixed with fish, chicken or beef? Maybe? Whatever we ate, we were thankful, and kept in mind that it was all part of the pilgrimage.

Communication. That was hard, staying in contact with other pilgrims. And if we split up into smaller groups, we tried to be on time, whether for work, dinner, shopping, etc. Not easily done in a place like India, where somebody always got lost, due to crowds, foreign language troubles, hard to distinguish environs, bad directions. It was important to be flexible, not panic and be patient.

Shower and Wash. In the winter season in Calcutta, personal laundry became quite the issue. All clothes were hand-washed in the bathroom next to the toilet. Often, I would wash while taking a shower (multi-tasking is an art during pilgrimages!). You're probably used to soft, bright clothes, but in India, while clean, they ended up looking rather crumpled. I'd get a bucket, soap, turn on the shower; wash body and head, make sure my suds dripped into the bucket, but not anywhere else. Then I'd pull clothes out of the bucket for rinsing, wring things out and hang them on the clothesline. Quite a feat to do all this without letting anything fall into the toilet or touch that horrible floor! I always had to avoid getting too cold, keeping my feet clean (no mats). A meticulous process, but something I got used to, especially thinking of the alternative – taking a shower outside on the streets like most urban Indians did, at a fire hydrant.

Flex plans. Almost daily, our plans went afoul. Indian people in general think differently than westerners, tons of talented people with the enervation of New York City but lacking in efficiency at times. When you say to some Indian folks, "Let's meet at 3p.m. for our program," adjust for arrival around 3.15, 3.30 or even later. You must concede to their way of doing things. Bend or break. Indian ways are more spontaneous and serendipitous than ours.

When you get into a taxi and state your destination, you may get out immediately, because the driver hasn't a clue where you want to go or nervously express it. And if you do get somewhere in a taxi, whether a few blocks or across town, expect to argue about the fare. I learned to haggle from my father (he was a salesman), and my take: it's the principle, not the actual price, and I pressed my case over fifty cents, determined not to be ripped off! If you order food on the street – like bargaining with the cook – in the end, your deal may break down. Be ready, flexible.

We don't always want to accept what is tough, challenging, difficult or different from our expectations as part of God's Plan- what God wills. That is, what He wants and desires – are part of His *passive will* and *active will*. God's *passive will*, this means it's what He *allows*, not necessarily what He wants or directs. God's *active will* is what He directs and guides. As limited human beings, we cannot always tell if a particular event is active or passive, but it does seem as if God puts up with a lot of passive stuff.

When we left for our pilgrimage, we obviously had much planned, but a lot that happened was unplanned. In the heat of the battle, one rolls with the punches, as there isn't time to determine what you're experiencing is active or passive. India is a place –and an adventure, so while there, even if you can't determine God's will perfectly, at least try getting into the "neighborhood," whether in India or anywhere else.

What you wanted to see. There's always sightseeing when traveling, even on "pilgrimage," so you want to make the best of where you are, since you may never pass that way again. But keep telling yourself: *It's a pilgrimage, not a holiday.* Keep your focus: *I'm here to serve. Be with the other pilgrims. Don't do exceptionally touristy things.* The reality is, you do see a lot of suffering and poverty. It makes you think. *Did I really want to do this?* And you (hopefully) answer: *Yes, these aren't "feel-good" experiences, but perhaps what God wanted me to see.*

When the system breaks down in a place like India, government response is unfortunately not always quick or well-organized, and not what you'd expect as an American. In Bengal State, after a strike, they shut down *everything*. Calcutta looked like a ghastly ghost-town. I shudder to think what would happen should there be an earthquake! So many Indian buildings are more like shacks; an earthquake would seemingly level most of Calcutta, like what happened in Haiti in 2010.

In India, chaos and suffering are replayed daily, multiplied by a billion with intensity and immensity, so perhaps there's communion between the two. We Christians usually have a lot of faith and can often simply bend the knee to pray and may ask questions, sometimes thinking: *Is God hiding?* Just don't stay in this mental position for too long.

So, think: Mother Teresa had been in spiritual darkness, and seemingly asked: *Where are you, God? I can't feel, sense or think of you, so please come soon and help.* Yet it seems we can never get a total "knock-out answer" to those sticky questions, and: *Why is there such wretched suffering allowed by an all-good God?* In the end, we've got to have faith, *trust*. Hit the ground running, storm heaven and pray. Don't think/don't blink, simply kneel and pray/don't get destabilized by doubt, get it out, or it will impair you. Hopefully, such doubts will humanize you without killing you and your faith life. In India, I felt both of these opposing impulses: Kneel and pray right away and to question. *Is God hiding?* All the volunteers, Mother Teresa, and the poor don't get stuck in their heads, but go on, with amazing faith.

What are the responses of a Christian? Go to Haiti or India? Yes, if that is what pleases God and what He wants. However, don't let a "giant missionary mandate" prevent you from seeing what's under your spiritual nose. Meaning: serve God, serve the poor and needy in the present moment, today, where God allows you the most time and accessibility. Sure, like great saints and missionaries, we all need bravado – a heroic "just do it"-attitude. Diss the doubt/kneel it out, pray and follow Him Who is the Way. He suffered, Himself, and in inviting solidarity, showed us the way. Relive His story –all the joys and sorrows. It's an ongoing imprinting way of Divinization –learning how God loves through the harshest ways: through suffering.

When Mother Teresa was deathly sick in 1993, there was a "spiritual campaign" to pray for her. After receiving an award in Delhi, with her bad heart, she couldn't return to her beloved Calcutta. On one of those days, I was serving in Kalighat (also known as "Mother's First Love," the Home for the Dying) and took time for prayer, went upstairs and saw a sister praying in front of the altar. The Missionaries of Charity were all taking time – throughout the entire world – to pray for their

Mother, taking vigil-rounds in front of the blessed Sacrament, and serving the poor.

Right there I witnessed a lone sister praying in front of the altar, kneeling on the bare floor, hands folded, rapt in attention to Jesus the Christ – the Holy Eucharist. I was stunned, as in front of her was a three-foot-high painting – one of the most striking I've ever seen. It was rather Mother-Teresa-ish, very old-world, gritty. On the bottom of the picture was a saying: "I looked for someone to help me," and, after that: "Be the one." It showed Jesus, hands tied and dangling in front of him, his entire body lacerated with cuts and wounds – horrific, even offensive – you could barely look at the Man without wincing, all bloody.

The Crucified Christ was wearing a crown of thorns and *that* would surely elicit sentiment. It brazenly reminds the viewer of the cost – and the nature – of Divine love. We don't usually think of love that way. We don't need a lot of excuses, consolations or philosophies spoken, or doubts settled: Simply love. That is what Mother Teresa did, even amidst doubts and blackouts. If you have a question? Love anyway. Got some person bugging you? Love anyway Been through an earthquake – physically or emotionally? Love anyway.

I'm sure anyone reading this account of my travels in India may ask The Question: How can God allow all this? Here are some responses…

1. Sin exists and the world is falling apart. Not only that, Satan attacks and accelerates the chaos. This is the foundation of all theodicy, admittedly lacking in so much conversation about it perhaps because it is seemingly embarrassing, part of a bygone fossilized faith. God allows some things and like Job, sent him some suffering (this is definitely not politically correct today). Put simply: God didn't plan things this way. Things are falling apart. Sometimes dramatically.
2. "But where sin increased, grace overflowed all the more" (Rm. 5:20). God allows suffering and evil, so that good may come of it, which is God's passive Will. This is St. Paul's dictum and teaching. It is in the Bible to remind us and leverage our lower

self into higher understanding. This can be easily misunderstood and ignorantly telecasted willy-nilly to untrained ears –coming off as callous. You've got to watch how when you say this to people – pastoral care is needed; timing is everything.

3. "Christ also suffered for you, leaving you an example that you should follow in his footsteps" (I Pt. 2:21) – we find here a pattern of Divinity – voluntary exposure to the world and evil means vulnerability, surrender and these are essentially part of God's showing of Himself. As a friend said to me, if God could have chosen some other way to show His love He would have. But as it is. He chose such cruel suffering to show us His depths.

These are the Grand Truths of Theodicy (the explanation of suffering). Sometimes we can understand one strand of this, and at another time another strand, or all three together. But still, it doesn't always make sense to us. I recently read in a book review: *God doesn't want us to understand Him, but to love Him.* In such times, we believers need not be irrational but *trans*-rational – the "answers" to suffering are not always rational and fly above reason's grasp to convey. It's not non-sense but religious faith – which is not always immediately-sensible, tangible.

The same is true of India. The upside of the "American take" is a "just do it" mentality, where true grit takes us through life and we overcome any obstacle, problem or disaster (Katrina and New Orleans are unfortunate exceptions). The downside? To surrender is difficult. This, or, our response, can all be corralled under the banner of "It's All Part of the Pilgrimage". Part of life is moving on. Don't be stuck. Get on with it. Indian mentality is far from American thinking sometimes, but also, like a lot of things, closer than we may think.

CHAPTER 4

It is the heart that gives. The hands merely let go.
-African Proverb

Giving is Receiving

GIVING & SERVICE

It's a way to become selfless. God certainly presents us with all kinds of opportunities to "give ourselves away". Just as long as we don't become rabid activists, let's focus on classic spirituality. The soul seeks completion, union, communion, and will get it somehow – by way of light (genuine friendships) or darkness (materialism, pornography). Directed charity is power not spent on self but rather a giving-away of things and time. Like the Good Samaritan (Luke Chapter 10) we are moved by compassion to help an-other. The soul will fulfill itself through good ways or be distorted through harmful ones. Its powers are realized in heaven with God the Trinity resting in Him, and with so many others (the saints) – Ultimate Communion. Traditionally, these "directive powers" are unleashed and fulfilled through contemplation: Resting in God, and through service, love of God and love of neighbor.

Here then is another way to appeal to modern man's desire to help: serving, giving, donating, a "rescue" of your soul is being exercised, the heart becomes liberated and spiritual desires are fulfilled. This may smell of self-interest, but it's disinterested in other ways. We cannot always articulate it, especially many Americans who want to give, for whatever reason.

Service took us to strange places – a leper colony (yes, they still exist, but are not called that anymore). Service was in many forms: Changing adult men's diapers, teaching children at a school in Darjeeling, singing songs to the poor.

As we fed others, *we* were being fed – spiritually and in other ways. This describes the spiritual paradox, learning new things in ways the rational person cannot always articulate, nor can we always penetrate God's mysterious ways, sometimes disguised. And then, there is the "coincidence of opposites" (i.e., Virgin-Mother, Jesus Who is God-Man, sinners who are graced).

We need always be open to learning and loving, yet, sadly, we are sometimes closed and sterile. The soul doesn't grow if it's closed off; it is meant to be expansive, encompassing and communing.

"It is in giving that we receive." -St. Francis of Assisi

The irony is that "giving is receiving" seems counter-intuitive, especially since humans usually want to gain. Yet, somehow, innately, we believe what St. Francis said to be true, mostly because St. Francis said it! He received a lot – sainthood, the stigmata, many followers, acknowledgements, all good.

At some level, Catholic-Christians believe that if we give like St. Francis, we will somehow receive and be rewarded. *And*, we know deep down that when we give, we go out of ourselves, give away and open up, that at sometime and somehow, we will receive in return. "Reap what you sow" as the saying goes. Now, if I add to this mix the American spirit of giving, one can cultivate something like a "consciousness of giving to receive". It becomes a mindset, and not just "doing" something, to be merely doing.

This might be describing the "magic" or "mysticism" of giving, giving an air of certain uncertainty and the immeasurability to the whole concept.

When we met a family on the street – literally living on the pavement right beside Mother Teresa's Motherhouse – we gave them rosaries, food and rupees. We were Americans doing our job: Seeking the poor and feeding the hungry and yet *they* were smiling and exuding joy; *they* showed thankfulness and silently preached to *us* the liberality and freedom of poverty. While feeling that *we* are the givers, we became receivers. There is no book, saint or person who can demonstrate this more than the poor themselves, they liberate one's soul from an impounded body and free you into new life. This is true spirituality. So, we can give with many mixed motives but the best reason, ultimately, Jesus the Master to Whom we give, existing mysteriously in that person standing in rags before you.

Life sometimes sends us challenges. We won't know what hit us, but sooner or later, we'll learn from that event. Oppositely, if someone tried to teach us a lesson in a familiar, more prosaic way, we might not learn. So many times, we learn more by irony, surprises, tragedies and paradoxes –in other words, through the "spiritual back door". When Jesus entered the apostles' conversation, as they argued over who would be greatest among His followers, He threw them His curveball. "The greatest among you must be your servant" (Mt. 23:11). Sometimes we get the lesson right away.

PEOPLE LOVED SERVING IN CALCUTTA – OTHERWISE, WHY WOULD THEY BE THERE?

Some travelers go to Calcutta for a week, or two (like we did), some for only a few days. Others went to Calcutta for a month, all summer, or for a whole year. They were passionate about the City of Joy, serving the poor and immersing themselves in *Calcutta-ness*.

Catholics are not drab disciples – they love loving – physically, spiritually and communally – so for them, love is pleasurable, passionate and purposeful. While we should realize (hopefully!) that love is of the will – it is a *conscious choice*. Love is also *eros* – passion, affection, filled with sentiments, and emotionally explosive. This "Catholic way" of loving exists because, well, it *is* biblical. I saw this in the many people we met in India, and in many non-Catholics. Giving helps a person come out of one's self, and gives a certain energy and synergy one can share with others.

***Amor facit exstasans*–** love produces ecstasy. Stand outside yourself (the literal meaning of ecstasy) through an ultimate experience into a new way of being. As a human being, you are attracted to loving and to others because you are free; you want to give yourself to the "other" – whether in a romantic relationship, charitable giving, or platonic friendship. Passion, affection – we all need these in life in the right ways. While spending time in Calcutta isn't for everyone, being there evokes and elicits passion, hopefully affection and sparks people to come out of themselves.

If you want to keep it, give it away. Jesus did, so why not you? This is the opposite of selfish love, or "*What's in it for me?*" Christ-like-Love tends to diffuse itself – it is outgoing and overflowing. I once heard some pilgrims say how much they loved visiting the clients of a drug treatment center – to inspire them, teach them, even learn from them and, most especially, simply to BE with them. Their love naturally overflows to be given away, and helps heal souls.

Bonum diffusm est *–good is diffusive of itself.* The more we love, the more we realize some boundaries of love are egotistical and barriers to God's Kingdom and His people. When we see others to whom we are attracted, then we too are inspired into a new way of being, and one can hope it's for the good. When I was with Father Sunil, our host, I emulated him in many ways. He was amazing. I'd love to ride a motorcycle all over the city like him, serve Mass and other forms of spirituality in many different venues, and I'd like to possess his gung-ho love of service and spirituality, and be action-oriented. I'm still trying!

Contraception. A "sticky issue" regarding the Missionaries of Charity. Their outreach program *is* about contraception, but not the way you think. Contraception is almost an accepted "incidental," a loud-yet-unspoken tactic of many (at least some) Western poverty outreach programs in India. It has become part of many peoples' lifestyles and has caused controversy within other foreign cultures. Not so with the Missionaries of Charity's aims. They have preserved Mother Teresa's desire for openness to new life in marriage, thereby promoting a not-so-subtle protest against some un-named multi-national companies that profit from toxifying the poor. To be fair, not all western aid organizations are like this.

For the MC's view on things, intimacy leads to ecstasy. When spouses in marriage become openly and physically loving, they literally give their insides to each other, contracepting nothing, and conceive children, hopefully making a deeper bond between the two spouses. From God's hard-wired design, we have two purposes of marriage – children and intimacy. Because of the shared, natural-loving intimacy – an intertwining and an emergence – this leads to an overflowing of love and life. The Indian culture understands this (yes, you see many families with lots of kids) and yet it is threatened with the contraceptive mentality that comes over with some westerners who mean well, but are not Hindu, and really don't get it. What I have seen in my time in India is indeed a clash of cultures, whether intended or not, and remains an unresolved issue.

Service. Here's a sacred story about St. Vincent DePaul (1581-1660), the French priest of the poor and of outstanding holiness: Apparently one time he was interrupted during a holy hour (prayer in church before the Blessed Sacrament of Jesus) by a beggar. Some attendants were surprised he'd would pause his holy hour for this man. The Saint then said, "I'm leaving Jesus to go *to* Jesus". He understood that Jesus is always in our midst under many guises, and not all of them are obvious.

Things don't always have to be "serious". Sometimes humor and holiness go together. When I was in Calcutta, every day, several dozen pilgrims went to morning Mass at Mother Teresa's Convent and then had *chai* – that is, Indian-esque tea. There we met lots of mostly-younger folks from all over the world; we shared in religious revelry with stories of our homelands. It was like a big, daily party after Mass! Then we would all a barnstorming-yet-spiritual song about serving Jesus and then head out onto the streets to serve a hundred poor, disabled adults at Prem Dan across town. So, service is not always somberly serious. Our pilgrims really got into the groove, and enjoyed it thoroughly. Like St. Vincent DePaul, they left Jesus after Mass to meet Him on the street.

What is poverty? I've learned so much from the many perspectives of people during my priesthood – and in India, I learned much about poverty. A pilgrim once wrote: "Isn't it funny that we travel great distances to see and experience 'poverty'". I spent time in Haiti one year, to see, touch and smell human poverty. We are such concrete individuals that we have to see, touch, smell it a certain way in order for our minds to believe. Poverty looks like this, "x," and when I see "x" then I understand that to be poverty. But when I see "y" then I don't see "poverty" because my brain is hard-wired to understand "x"= poverty. Yet our own country suffers from poverty to the maximum degree: Moral poverty, ethical poverty, spiritual poverty, etc. There is so much need in our own country. Poverty presents itself in a different way than how we think it looks, yet it is right in front of us. People "appear" happy and healthy on the outside and yet inside there is such suffering. Suffering is disguised by careers, progress, materialism, sensuality etc.

Ghandi-Ji Leprosarium. It seemed to be the hottest day of our time in India, walking across the train tracks, and on each side, the ground was covered by drying cow dung, simmering in the sagacious sun. And amidst all this in the distance we saw the lepers reaching out to us as we visited. We sang and prayed for them.

I asked one of the workers there: "What is most fulfilling work you do here?" His response: "It's a privilege to serve here. It's a once-in-a-lifetime opportunity." Totally inspiring, and I was perhaps even a bit stunned. Most people don't always see things that way, often being too busy. Some may see service work as, well, just that — work, something to do or get *through*, certainly not something to enjoy. This man serving at the leprosarium awed me, he must be gifted by God, to project such a beautiful spirit, or it could be something he learned along the way. *I want to be like him, and feel about things the way he does,* was my thought. And, in a way, I began growing toward gaining this sense of service. Whether he realized it or not, that man gave me the inspiration to live another way.

After some thought, I concluded there are three types of people.

#1-Those who are gifted and lifted, naturally freed from selfishness to serve — it's their "first nature". This kind of saintly soul is graced and inspiring!

#2-There are those who learn this art of selflessness (and its ability to free the spirit), so serving gradually becomes a "second nature".

#3-Lastly, there are those who struggle with service, who may not possess a giving nature, nor can they ever feel freed enough to give at all, and thus become stuck, dealing with numerous personal obstacles keeping him-or-her from serving, and give up, thinking there is too much to overcome.

Perhaps many of us have lived through one or all of these stages of service. Could a person grow from #3 toward #1? Could I become like the man at the leprosarium? All things are possible, but to get into that second-nature to first-nature groove, maybe. One thing is certain: it takes extremely hard work to move away from #3. One must be willing to take risks, keep imitating the saints, giving until it hurts, and "give anyway," loving and letting go.

Why Serve? Family relationships and communication problems are real, dramatic and, sometimes visceral. We need help sometimes, and for some, counseling is necessary. As one pilgrim said once, in order to get a proper perspective is to look at the present problem in light of the whole. In other words, see the "big picture" as in "thinking globally". Maybe that's why we met so many volunteers in Calcutta. They wanted to get a grip on their own problems by serving Jesus in His suffering – it reminded them of what was real and important. They wanted to see and experience another's suffering, and then could re-visit their own issues afresh, and finally detach from the selfish absorption of navel-gazing and existentialism. Only then could they be freed.

Serving in India was a challenge in other, more basic ways, especially when one cannot speak the native language. A cultural bridge separates you from "them". So, I had to resort to using exaggerated hand gestures and facial expressions, and sometimes it worked. Communication and/or connection can take unusual forms. A pilgrim described an incident while serving at North Point, the children's Jesuit school in Darjeeling. She was trying to relate basic facts of life with the kids, have an elevated discourse, and things wouldn't jibe, very frustrating. She wanted to speak of lofty things, but the only thing they had in common was *American Teen Idol!* So, the moral of the story – communication will happen, but in ways you don't expect.

Varanasi / Benares - The ghats where cremations take place on the Ganges River

COMMITMENT

In Darjeeling, we met Sister Joan, of the Loreto religious order (Institute of the Blessed Virgin), who was celebrating 50 years in service. She was probably the most hospitable and spiritual person I'd yet met on our journey. She had just completed a five-day retreat and was sparkling, spiritually speaking, so I asked if we could make a retreat at "her place" – the religious house where she lived (the same place Mother Teresa made her transformative retreat and underwent a deeper conversion—her "call within a call" to eventually found the Missionaries of Charity). Sister Joan said "Yes", eyes gleaming, and also said that she would pray for us!

On arrival, we saw a photo of a baby boy in the common room, sitting on the fireplace mantle, clearly a place of honor. Sister Joan told us the story. This boy had been left mysteriously in a nearby jungle, covered by moss, insects and filth, barely alive. He was brought to a Darjeeling orphanage where a heroic British lady took in the baby, nursed and eventually adopted him. That baby fought for life, only a few months old, ended up in a hospital, but didn't make it. The manager of the orphanage came to Sister Joan, and tearfully asked if the sisters and church could host the baby's funeral. Sister Joan immediately said "Yes, of course." Hundreds of people honored the child's brief life and dignified death. We should all give of our emotional and material goods, especially to the most-outcast, to the most-vulnerable, and especially to the very young.

We saw in Sister Joan's shining soul an extraordinary commitment, heroic charity and Love, all that comes with physical sacrifice – which is part of the seriously-committed to a religious life. Fifty years and still going strong! I was struck by her literal poverty – the rooms where she lived were cold and drafty. She always wore gloves. Once, Sister Joan mentioned that bats sometimes flew around the house, speaking as though they were no more than flies – totally unruffled. I thought: *I complain about getting a sniffle and this holy lady troops through this place with dedicated zeal in cold-dampness and constant cloudiness.* Humbling.

TOO MUCH 'I'?

Over my years of service, I've occasionally needed purification of myself and my motives, as I begin seeing too much of *me*. We all have mixed motives – we serve others because, at least subtly, we're getting some fulfillment while helping a needy person. That's human nature and reality, right? But then there are mixed-up motives – an infusion-confusion of excessive ego, lots more than necessary, when it's a calling-attention to myself rather than serving humbly and anonymously.

I recall a lady who worked in a leprosarium with the Jesuits at Mardighara. She'd been there 25 years, constantly smiling and joyful. There were no pictures or trophies acknowledging her service, but the opposite – ongoing demand, terrible smells and people with constant needs, challenges, difficulties and darkness. *I* want adulation and to be in the limelight, but she works, day-in and day-out, with giant challenges, and smiles all the time.

There are many anonymous souls in Calcutta who were far humbler than I, are they perhaps more holy? If we serve for self-gratification and personal fulfillment, then what's the use? Do I want to serve strictly for bragging-rights back home? Do I go to India for my own fulfillment? Do I travel on pilgrimage because *I* want to feel good, or do I want someone *else* to feel good?

The ladies of our pilgrimage group worked upstairs at Prem Dan without complaint, out of view and removed from the circulation, beauty and spaciousness of the courtyard, and in squalid surroundings. One held in her arms a lady so poor she couldn't do anything for herself but clutch her baby close. That's selflessness I don't have.

A lot of times, especially in India, I *have* to admit it. I was in this service for personal feel-good vibes, as in: "I'll do this for a while, then go back home to my comfortable place." *Hmm… time for a spiritual re-group.* My (new) goal is to be in it more for Jesus and the person served than for myself. Slowly – ever so slowly perhaps – I'll progress from selfishness and achieve more selflessness.

I remain a work-in-progress.

CHAPTER 5

"Teach us to give and not count the cost."
- St. Ignatius de Loyola

Roll with The Punches

Pilgrimage in India is not exactly compatible with Type-A personalities – if you're wound too tight, the fluid and changing nature of Indian life will be a challenging experience. If you're uncomfortable eating strange food, then Indian cuisine will patently terrify you. If being around thousands of people who don't speak English puts you on edge, you decided to go there, so deal with it. Listen with your heart, watch with your soul's eyes, and with your mouth closed. Being amenable and extraordinarily adaptable is absolutely essential to survive *and thrive* on pilgrimage anywhere – especially in India.

Go on pilgrimage with a plan that's not too rigid; however, being too haphazard has its drawbacks, too. It's a balance between *planning and spontaneity*. One of the biggest differences between East and West: The spontaneity and careening cacophony that is Eastern and so very Indian, contrasted with the conveyor-belt-like control (like obeying traffic rules!) in the West. Somewhere between these extremes, there is truth and balance! Life in general – and India in particular – requires "go-with-the-flow" personalities who can roll with the chaos of train stations, bartering with vendors and finally taking that much-needed siesta. There's a different spirit at work there, so be open, but not so rigid that you'll straitjacket the Spirit.

CALCUTTA GREEN…*NOT!*

If you think greenhouse gases in the U.S. are bad, then you shouldn't go to Calcutta for any length of time. The air is challenging. There are tons of cars and taxis – without catalytic converters – belching toxins, smoky motor scooters zipping through traffic willy-nilly, along with factories spewing who-knows-what fumes into the atmosphere. The constant pollution will make your lungs and sinuses put up quite a fight, and yes, it's health-threatening. You'll cough a lot, and endure a constant case of the sniffles. And of course, there's trash everywhere. Almost anything can become a garbage dump.

Open-air fires are everywhere, and all year around – with people baking pecans, rice and meat, or burning litter, which *really* smells bad. No regulations exist regarding fires; few seem to care, as long as the fires are under control. Plus, there are few "green areas" or parks to counteract this vast city's fine art of polluting. This is not the place for anyone with breathing issues (asthma or emphysema, for instance).

Calcutta is a sea of concrete covered by masses of people and permeated with semi-toxic air. What was the view from my room? A family sleeping on the street right below my window, amongst piles of trash.

That is the real Calcutta, and if you're there for pilgrimage, roll with it. If you can get through the first 48 hours, then you'll do well for the long haul.

GETTING ALONG

When traveling with a group, it's a hope that everyone will be compatible with one another. It's not always a given, but I was delighted how amenable everyone was in our particular pilgrimage.

So, is the vibe really that good on pilgrimage all the time? Not always. Think about it: If you go with your family to the beach for a holiday, you're in close quarters more than usual, you'll start getting on each other's nerves. Plus, as one pilgrim pointed out, while on vacation: "You'll notice things about family members you don't notice other times at home." Hmmm, so true.

Most pilgrims are obviously not bad-tempered as a rule, basically they are pre-packaged with an amiable temperament – able to get along, overlook faults and be spiritually- and charitably-inclined toward the common good and are all about teamwork. But here's a caveat: People are people, things happen that will push buttons; deeper, less-pleasant personalities may be revealed under stress. No matter how spiritual someone is, she/he can grate on another person's nerves. Be sensitive to this aspect, if you are a manipulative button-pusher who likes head games, don't go on pilgrimage.

Needed on any pilgrimage: Open hearts, mindfulness to remember who we are (gnarly pilgrims), and that we are missionaries with no exit strategy, except to make it through the trip together. Be patient in all things, don't make mole-hills into mountains, stay upbeat as much as possible; as despair and a negative attitude will ruin the pilgrimage for everyone.

When a pilgrim has a disagreement, an upset or a personal trial, try, as a fellow sojourner, to learn from it. Of course, being with a group in close quarters for an extended period might engender "cabin fever" – you might feel suffocated and get the blues. But, as pilgrims, we are committed to sticking together for two weeks and can't steam independently. Whatever the problem, the group must work it out together.

Those are lessons of life— anywhere, anytime.

Down and out? During our tour of the Jesu Ashram Leprosarium, I noticed about a third of our group disappeared during different parts of the tour. Perhaps it was because of the heat getting to them, the sights (how many very-sick people without hands or eyes can you endure in one visit?), the environment (seriously-bad B.O., heavy air, severe sickness and overwhelming sadness) or, more simply, compassion-fatigue finally set in, exacerbated by sheer exhaustion.

Our program in the Jesu Ashram was go on the tour, led by a guide. We had to acknowledge the sick and suffering clients, keep smiling, sing a song, and then greet each individual and, if possible, talk with them – this with the all-too-obvious communications gap (doubly so, many clients, because of leprosy, couldn't see, hear or verbalize). Each volunteer had to try really hard to make up for those limitations, this was wearing on them, when it was obvious communication wasn't working. We pilgrims were running out of gimmicks. This took "rolling with the punches" to an extreme, with people trying almost anything until something worked and when it didn't, we had to keep moving – often with a spirit of detachment(and some humor).

Liberation theology? We'd spent several days at North Point, location of a Jesuit school just outside of Darjeeling. It is a haven, an oasis of calm, order and near-opulence, by Indian standards. The architecture, sprawling grounds, and décor were all very impressive and so opposite from the poverty elsewhere in India.

Father Kinsley, head of the North Point complex, explained that it used to be an elite school, where the Jesuits taught kings and princes of northern India, Bhutan and Nepal and other nobility, but now the school was for everybody. I had to ask myself: *Is this what you would call Jesuit liberation theology?* I got a whiff that this is exactly what it was the Jesuits and their associates (all laypersons) are very sincere, and seemed to be doing a good job. The boarders and daily attendees at North Point were mostly poor, i.e., from the lower castes. One might call this school the "Harvard of the Himalayas", and was open to all kinds of people who have no money, a respectable, holy and very-Jesuit thing to do.

Accidents Happen. On our trip from the Calcutta airport in 2009 – at three in the morning – we were traveling in three SUVs, enjoying the new smoggy-foggy smells (yes, I'm being sarcastic) and environs, looking at most mesmerizing scenery, that is, run-down houses, wandering animals, and chaotic neighborhoods. After a thirty-minute bumpy ride, we arrived safely at our destination – Our Lady of the Seven Dolors – buuuut, we were minus one SUV. Apparently, it had broken down. We were missing seven pilgrims. Just a minor detail? Ahhhh… no. After traveling a few thousand miles, only to lose nearly half of the group ten miles from our destination? Several phone calls and many prayers later, everyone arrived, and all in one piece. Instant relief, with no need to panic. Everything was back on track. Let's just say, it made for an interesting beginning of our pilgrimage, giving us an idea of what was to come, and to be flexible.

Same body, different country. My pilgrimage in 2009 changed for me. *How*? As mentioned much earlier, I'd torn a muscle in my leg, racing barefoot. Not my best move. I paid for it with pain and swelling. This turned out to be a personal challenge, as I usually take my good health for granted, and tend to explode out of the gate without thinking – and with some over-estimation of my capabilities. So, through the rest of the pilgrimage, I adjusted my activity, laying off the bad leg, sitting more, avoiding certain movements, trying to do my own self-therapy.

While this was uncomfortable, it was far from unbearable – especially compared to being in Calcutta. Being wounded or sick has never been easy for me, and certainly seemed worse while on pilgrimage. But I'd already seen people with leprosy, AIDS, tuberculosis, no eyes, broken limbs or starving on the streets – no way would I complain about my temporary discomfort.

"Don't stay there". This is so important. It's about thinking right, or better. While visiting a lady one time who was elderly and sick and a daily mass-communicant, I asked her about getting better, and she replied: "Well, Father, I'm an optimist. I don't believe in self-pity and all that. But I guess not getting well for a while crosses my mind". But, she continued, "I don't stay there." While she was shrewd and spiritual, she was also realistic, and admitted to thinking difficult thoughts – or at least having them from time to time. We need to combine spiritual and shrewdness in our lives, make a decision to stay or *not-stay* in a certain mind-state. Dark negativity can overwhelm us, even as we try to climb out of that pit. As I heard once at an Alcoholics Anonymous meeting: *Misery is optional*. Yet, as much as we try, sometimes we have that "Velcro experience" – being stuck on bad thoughts, but like someone said, "I can't stay there." It really is, a lot of times, a choice.

I remember back in 1993 in Calcutta, when I volunteered at Kalighat. It was the afternoon – usually a slow time when few volunteers were around. I heard racket, went to check it out and saw a few Indians bringing in someone through the front door. There were cries for the head of the house, and Sister Luke appeared. They laid the man down on a makeshift stretcher; and the guy looked like he might be dying. The shrieks of the men carrying him finally stopped. When they turned the man over, there was a hole in his back. Yes, a fist-sized hole, blood coming out and globular stuff, too! Sister Luke was undeterred; she jumped in and took a look – turned out she was a nurse and knew what to do. I winced, took a breath, fixated on my own struggles while she and others went to work saving this man's life. Turns out he'd been thrown out – castaway in a gutter and left to die. Now, if he *was* going to die, then it would be in dignity and peace; after all, he was at Mother's First Love, where Mother Teresa most commonly said: "One should die in dignity, not like a dog."

Fake it Till You Make it. I learned that phrase from a friend, while he was undergoing sobriety via the 12- step program. What I drew from that? Sometimes, you have to train your brain, or even override it. When your body and soul start to drag or doubt, you must hijack your ego, lower your basic self until you've learned how do things in a new way, and then stay in that new groove. Those new actions have to become second nature to you; it's hard work to maintain, until those new, unfamiliar motions feel normal. This is life, even if not on pilgrimage in India!

There's a Franciscan priest, Brother Solanus Casey, who once dispensed pretty significant spiritual counsel: "Thank God ahead of time." Translation: Abandon all to Divine Providence. Thanking God before all events is to trust in His providing for you. Not simple. I had to trust a lot in God's providing-providence without actually knowing the exactness of the details. As said earlier, the best action in such circumstances: *Fake it till you make it!*

Putting things in perspective, maybe there are spiritual stages we as Catholic-Christians should recognize, such as: 1-Just hanging on. 2-Surviving by a wing and a prayer. 3-Praying the aspiration: "Jesus I trust in you" at all times. 4-Trusting in God so much *and* thanking God ahead of time. While not knowing all that's ahead, that saying has helped me. So, remember: Thank God ahead of time.

It's Who You Know. As I mentioned earlier, our host Father Sunil had all kinds of trips and plans for us in and around Calcutta. We went to convents, shrines, soup kitchens, more convents and various other places we didn't know about until we arrived. He was a master planner and an overseer dad-type who had all the connections and at the same time, a concern for us as his spiritual children. I'm not sure things would have been at all pleasant, organized or even possible if he hadn't been there. Father Sunil was our "boots on the ground" guy and made a lot of good things happen. In other applications of life: if you know someone in an area where you want to get a job, that person might get your foot in the door. If you know someone at the party, you'll feel more comfortable. If you know someone in Heaven then… Q.E.D. (*quod erat demonstandum,* meaning, "that which was to be demonstrated").

Darjeeling. Wow, it was cool there. Not outside – semi-spring-like in the sunshine – but inside our residence, the Jesuits' home, no, not cool. It was *cold*, with a dampness that got under your skin and stayed there. The most common thought was: *How am I gonna get warm?* This hung over you whether in the bathroom, getting ready for bed, washing, shaving or eating. The damp cold overrode other things, as your mind kept saying: *How can I do this activity and keep warm at the same time?*

After a while, I considered: *Should we get out of Dodge? Morale is down, somebody different is getting sick every day. Should we "cut and run"?* When I finally said that we'd be leaving a day early, people surprised me and said they were making the best of it, okay, okay, it was cold, but they were embracing the challenge, humbling, after all, "It's all part of the pilgrimage!" Hmm, really? But I didn't cave, said we should leave a bit earlier, and we did…

We secured lodgings down in Mardighara (below the mountains) with the Jesuits. In this "high altitude pinch" everyone helped out heroically, and eventually we made our way down the mountain – just after seeing splendid Kanchenjunga from a Darjeeling park. And it was then I re-thought: *Did I make the right decision to leave early? Could we have stayed just another day? But then, just look at the beauty of this mountain, and it is a lot warmer.* That's real life. Make a decision based on the best evidence you have at the time, even after getting other evidence after the fact. Regardless of what you decide to do, make it work.

Look at misfortunes as adventures. Whether being ripped off by a taxi driver, getting a headache, boarding an overcrowded bus, getting a bigger bill than expected—that's India. I had to look upon these difficulties as veiled lessons of love and wisdom, hard to accept with grace, that the more often those things happened, the more we will have peace, the more we will learn in life and ultimately be perfected. *Yeah, right.* I must be patient. So, I have to ask: *What is the good I can learn from this? What does God have for me wrapped up in this drama?* All I can say: Look for and remember that the cloud has a silver lining, somewhere!

ROCK AND ROLL WITH IT!

One of the funniest experiences came after our pilgrims had an evening discussion of music in the Mass. Someone mentioned that drums were okay for African folks since it's their native cultural expression, while in the West, we don't have that indigenous custom. I just listened.

Our Mass the next morning was at the Prem Dan Children's Center for the handicapped. We went early during a soft rainfall, began the Mass with an opening song, a Christmas carol. Three children played drums in the back of the chapel. A conspiracy-follow-up of our evening discussion to rattle or stimulate our souls? It sounded like a carnival, with clanging symbols, rattling drums and droning rhythm, like a religious oom-pah band. It sounded rough, but one child played with his one good hand, and another was blind, this made it all the more sincere. I saw it as a God-given in-your-face response to our theoretical discussion on music. Drum playing has its place, at times, discordant or melodic. Theory meets reality? Reality can shatter our theories when confronted with living truth. The lesson here: be ready to bend, adapt and learn anew.

PASSING THE TIME

Sometimes there were "non-activities". We needed down-time after non-stop service to others, and took our rare, free time to replenish spiritual fuel – an essential requirement along the Way.

What did we do? Some of us did nothing, gratefully. Others played soccer with the locals. I sat and watched, vicariously enjoying their zest and energy to play, even in that ever-present heat. Most enjoyed sitting around after an exhausting morning or afternoon, just talking, as fans twirled overhead trying to move the excessively-humid air. We simply passed the time, relaxing in one another's company. It was a different matter in Darjeeling, where we'd gather to rap in one room, door closed – just to stay warm!

Strolling and other activities. Other times, some walked around and shopped – for food, clothes, kitsch, crafts, gifts, somehow, even amidst the franticness of Indian streets, some pilgrims could actually relax. Not *my* idea of calming the body and soul! Of course, there was always reading. I brought far too many books, knowing I wouldn't get through everything.

And then the day came.

It was our last day of pilgrimage! Almost depressing, being at the end, but what was worse –having to wake up at 3:00 a.m. Time to finish packing, count noses, pull protesting late-sleepers out of bed, load luggage in taxi-trucks, and make it to the airport.

The next hurdle: unload the trucks, fight off intrepid entrepreneurs trying to make a buck from us, get through airport security, and then slog through a couple of long lines. At the same time, it was ghostly and frantic, only 4:00 a.m. and things felt surreal. Like zombies, we wandered through various lines, hit a Big One and it wasn't budging. People sat and slept. Big questions niggled at me: *Was it all worth it? Why did I do this? Am I gonna make it home?* No one gave voice to any somber thoughts. Waiting, and waiting, hoping. What's not happening? Bad vibes, people got out of line and approached the desk. *Not good.* Our flight had been cancelled—from excessive pollution. *Will we get another flight right away?* No. *Oh, boy. What now?*

Time for the next round, and it's a biggie: We must retrieve checked luggage and wandering pilgrims, that took a while. Then we were back outside, on the street, into more taxis, and on to the Oberoi Hotel. We arrived, but were stopped by the bomb squad, oookay. By now, it's 7:00 a.m. We were promised free meals and an overnight stay. This hotel was opulent, with gold-fauceted sinks and bathtubs, plush carpet and TV's and room service. Crazy! We had breakfast with the rest of the travelers – a hundred or so, in a common room and returned to our rooms. There had been no announcement of the next flight out, so we were exiled in paradise, two of us didn't sleep, but made calls, trying to find seats on any flight out of India for eighteen people. Here was The Debate – push onto fly out, or not? Yes, we'd push if necessary.

Finally, we negotiated and stitched together a plan: we'd leave Calcutta that evening, go to Germany and then to Dulles. Time to re-pack! Better a day late, then not at all. Here was the catch: We had to be at the airport soon for our flight – it was leaving in two hours! Somehow, we did it, after a lot of hurrying, worrying, and haggling.

We'd already spent two weeks rolling with the punches in India, changed what we could and accepted what couldn't be changed. *Was it worth it?* Yes. We all learned big Life Lessons, especially keeping cool during high-pressure situations.

Brick carrier...that's using your head. When we visited Mother Teresa's sprawling place in Calcutta, we passed an amazing sight: A building project within a gigantic hole, surrounded by partially-built sides of the building, and lot of other projects which were in seeming-disrepair and incomplete.

Within the one project, there was a makeshift crane with a large hammer at the end of a long rope which was used to pound stakes which would become shafts and foundations for the building. This gargantuan tool looked primitive, but it worked. A moment later, I saw a young man with a white cloth on his head and then he then put twelve bricks on top of his head, stacked them brick-by-brick and carried this huge load to the work site. Wow. He had a strong back, and considerable determination. Wow.

Could I do that? I tried carrying two bricks on my head and failed. I was missing something, my culture had nothing to tell me how to carry those things, but in India, such primitive-but-useful skills were still being taught. India is a paradox. It has a Silicon Valley of sorts, economic prowess which is among the world's strongest, but their centuries-old way of doing some things has never disappeared.

Paradoxes are everywhere. We look for consistency in life, and patterns and for our rational minds, which neutrally seek refuge against chaos, but it doesn't always work. And amidst poverty and chaos, there are rationalist-mantras that replay in our minds: *Can it be solved with modern technology? Can such crazy chaos be that hard to fix?* Maybe the big reason westerners don't like going east, the primitive lives alongside high-tech. Poverty lives on pavement in front of the opulent hotels. Too different, too stark, and it demands a response. Everyone wants to live a new, different life, but not everyone wants to change themselves too much, frightening in concept, that there's possibility to respond, to open themselves up to new life, when God calls you to change. What else is new?

Like those workers who resorted to primitive methods, and finished the job, they rolled with the punches. Likewise, so can we.

CHAPTER 6

"If you are what you should be, you will
set the whole world ablaze!"
-St. Catherine of Sienna

Adventure

Many Americans lust after excitement and ecstasy. Obviously, you don't have to travel to India for adventure. If you learn to see God's epiphanies in each present moment – miracles appear. That's the constant joy and wonderment of spiritual childhood Jesus speaks of: "For the kingdom of God belongs to such as these" (Lk. 18:16). Encounter God wherever we are, and cultivate zest on your quest! Seasoned travelers seek more new experiences, and want to explore unknown horizons.

And then there's India, where there are plenty of unknowns. As noted earlier, Calcutta smells VERY different; your entire body feels permeated by it all. It wasn't my first trip, so I knew what to expect. However, many travelers go to India totally unprepared: Some didn't know how use Indian bathrooms (sometimes a hole in the ground, or just next to a shower), that they'd have to haggle prices with cab drivers and had no idea Calcutta traffic would be insane. An Indian pilgrimage is fraught with extremes, many victories (meeting new people, learning strange customs, overcoming internal barriers) and crashing debacles (getting sick, burning out from pollution, seeing/dealing with constant poverty).If you've been on pilgrimage there, you know it's an adventure.

So, you'd better buckle up. India is SO different, it's an adventure to the max!

By definition, the word *adventure* literally means "to come to." In a new place, you have the opportunity to embrace a new self, a new way of being, one that may be foreign at first, but the more a person experiences during travel, the more it is welcomed, liberating and revealing.

Toto, we're not in Kansas anymore. Your first challenges: Getting through customs (while arguing with gun-toting guards) hearing unfamiliar accents, and being expected to follow procedures you don't understand – at two in the morning.

Next, just outside the airport, you'll see massive crowds. It will be unnerving… or exciting, depending on how you feel. Everything is "in your face" and quite shocking to first-timers. Getting into vehicles, traveling through dark streets, seeing wandering cows and open fires; people actually sleeping next to the road! And even if you can't see it, you will *smell* the tons of trash.

Finally, you arrive at your lodging; your heart is racing. Tell yourself: *Don't panic, be flexible.*

Tenacity. In 1993 while in Darjeeling, we met a Brit named Peter. Turned out he was a "wanted man"! Back story: Peter had gone alone to Calcutta to serve with the MCs at Kalighat, right out of the blue. Then, after a couple of weeks, he got sick, and with no notice, traveled to Darjeeling – according to him, to get out of the city for clean air and refreshment.

Thing is, everyone thought the worst, since he'd left no clues, Peter was assumed dead, perhaps abducted, even attacked. It took the Indian police two weeks to trace him to his hotel room in Darjeeling. After Peter and I laughed about this, we became friends, and over two days, we hung out with him.

Over dinner, he told us about an incident in Calcutta with the MCs. Apparently, they had come upon a body while out and about, a dying man, all alone. All they could do was take him to Kalighat, so he could die in dignity. Peter carried the man and commented, "It was as if I'd carried Jesus." The look on his face said everything.

Peter was so committed to service, perhaps because Mother Teresa was, and she inspired him to keep on serving. That's what's known as a 'chain reaction', to pass on a saint's legacy of love. Mother Seton (the first American-born saint) said this: "Hazard forward always." She lived this advice, after many losses, among them, a mother, husband, two daughters and other family members. We need this virtue in life, lest we become too easily defeated, losing vision and spirit.

Love, which Peter showed to me in a new way, is a *choice of the will*: Whether in marriage, commitment to the single life, a job, one's family, it turns out that sometimes love is not always pretty when the honeymoon is over, there are dark days that get us down. It's precisely through these troubled times we must consciously choose loving and to keep our commitments. The sooner and younger we learn this Lesson, the better – and the result? This will become a holy habit within ourselves.

Think of it as the **Three C's –C**onsciously **C**hoosing **C**hrist – and what He wants for us. That is what Peter showed mein such dramatic fashion. The opposite of this: Thinking that love is only a feeling or a pleasurable emotion; that love is not formed by choices but merely happens – like "falling for someone". The Three C's keeps us grounded, and from becoming addicted to the pleasure.

Thrill and Chill… to Darjeeling! The higher we got, the colder it became. The drive up the mountains was absolutely thrilling – it became a race of sorts among our three vehicles with guys and girls hanging out the windows, yelling and screaming. Those hairpin turns were scary, hair-raising! We stopped in Mardighara at a gas station with fast food – almost American-style. Adrenaline pumping, and still wired after our previous train ride from Calcutta, we loaded up on sweets and sodas. For this journey, we were true tourists and saw the sights. It wasn't a fast trip, and some parts of the road were very narrow – one-lane, and no shoulders. Often, we had to wait for oncoming traffic to pass. We saw valleys with houses perched over cliff sides, and, most amazing thing of all, was how close to the edge our vehicles got. Our drivers were totally focused –grimacing at times, yelling at other drivers, but always moving – the ultimate road warriors who brought us to a city on the hill.

Halfway into our journey, we stopped at a food mall to refuel ourselves, get cold drinks, catch our breaths, but didn't stay too long, we were exhausted, but still pumped, ready for more close calls and scenic vistas, going ever-higher. What a perilous and ennervating trip!

Poverty… as adventure? We got an extended, up-close and personal view of poverty on this pilgrimage. Indian poverty is right-in-your-face, explicit and everywhere –quite different from the U.S., where it seems to be contained in certain areas of cities, or concealed behind closed doors in the countryside. While poverty in India is at first glance atrocious, blatant and hard-hitting, but very similar to poverty in many third-world countries. A pilgrim may gradually befriend it, and in the public nature-spectacle, learn from it. There is no need of pretense or hiding one's station in life. Whether in the maddening traffic or among bustling pedestrians, there is an elegant cacophony and orchestration of the chaos which one learns, and maybe even appreciates. Maybe that is why Mother Teresa was more at home in Calcutta than anywhere else, she often decried the "poverty of the West."

At Red Fort near Taj Mahal, Old Delhi, central India

KISS: Keep It Simple, Saint

That's a lesson I must continue to learn – to keep things simple. During my first pilgrimage to Calcutta, I was maudlin at the end— my sabbatical was done, pilgrimage over, and I had to be back at work in a few days. So, I decided to take a chance and ask a saint for advice, meaning Mother Teresa: "So," I asked, "what should I do when I go back to a large parish? I will be leaving Calcutta, to wade through new waters. What do you suggest?"

Mother Teresa's advice: "Teach them to pray, to pray as a family."

Hmmm… I went to seminary for four years, and never learned some-thing so elemental-teaching people, and families, to pray. And a simple lady taught me this in a knee-jerk moment. Staggering. Where's the balance between doing what we need to do, and doing the first-and-foremost important things? Fifteen years later, I've veered off the path at times. I've gotten caught up on myself, and in doing unnecessary things. Remembering this sage advice put me back on the path.

Confrontation. One time when we went to Sutter Street for shopping, and later on to a mall, we encountered a difficult problem: We were being followed. No matter what, we couldn't shake the guys following us. This was an indoor mall with lots of stores, so we tried ducking into shops here and there, but these fellows were persistent. I confronted one of them, but he acted as though he didn't understand me, or at least, couldn't – or wouldn't– respond in English. At first, I thought they were thieves, then street kids, I couldn't figure out what they were. Finally, we asked someone and was told they were hired by the mall to "pursue business", whatever that meant. At any rate, they were tenacious and definitely good at their job! We moved on.

Addendum: *Northward!...*

Though I will not detail my trips to these places, Tibet and Kashmir, these were adventures way fun and thrilling that I recommend anyone while in India to go.

While in 1993, in Delhi, I happened to meet some nice folks who put me up for a huge discount. Further, they said they had connections to Kashmir and famed Dal Lake. I took them up on it and the next day I was on a plane north to Jammu and Kashmir, and a couple days of "cooling off" as it was obviously way different than the middle of India, in the plains. I got off the plane and headed toward Srinagar, the capital of the region and it was like a ghost town. I had walked into a gun fight, kind of. For many years India and Pakistan, Hindus and Muslims have been contesting the land and the prize possession Dal Lake and environs. So: I got the whole town and lake to myself and stayed a couple days in total relaxation and silence. Though it was a kind of eerie silence—a few days earlier there was a terrorist bombing—I enjoyed it nonetheless; most importantly it was cool. The green, fertile and moist atmosphere was healing ot my body and soul as I stayed on a house boat on the lake and took walks and hikes— and avoided terrorists! This was another adventure serendipity benefit, meeting those folks in Delhi and making up things as I went along!

Kind of likewise was my journey to Tibet, as I stayed with the Jesuits in Kathmandu and they taught how to get there. I went with a Spanish tour group and our first attempt was canceled by the Chinese government (as Tibet is now under this communist orbit) and so we had to stay in a hotel in Kathmandu before going the next day. We made it in to Lhasa, the famed capital, and were welcomed by Tibetans who gave us a white saffron veil. On our bus trip through the countryside to center city we saw marvelous Buddha statues cared into hillsides and small towns and, thankfully, bright sun as it was indeed, cooler.

I still recall playing basketball with Tibetans, the mighty-huge, golden Buddha statues in monasteries we visited and many monks who seemed always to be smiling. Lastly, I especially recall the aged monk who was going through Lhasa and doing penance: he would walk about ten feet, then slip down to his knees, and then to his face on the ground and do a full prostration. He would then stand and walk on another ten feet and repeat, doing this for blocks until we parted. He was not young. This showed me the fusion of religion and culture in the "Land of the Snows" and how reverenced the ancient religion is there.

I was so thankful for these two "add-on" trips which I neither foresaw nor could plan for ahead of time but which, Indian style, gifted me with opportunity and more adventure

CHAPTER 7

"If you are what you should be, you will
set the whole world ablaze!"
-St. Catherine of Sienna

Teamwork

While on pilgrimage in India, we emphasized the teamwork aspect, knowing we had to work together, and if one of us felt secure on his or her own, it was emphasized that a lone operator would be the only American in an ocean of Indians. This was a topic of discussion two or three times before our trip, mostly that it was important we work and travel always as a group, then stressed the importance of unity, communication and spending time together – on- and off-"duty". Something took, as once we got off the plane in Calcutta, we were already a spiritual team, rather than gawking individualists making it up as we went along, separating here and there. We were going to stick together.

One time, I got advice when I didn't want it. In Matagura, I was playing with about a hundred school kids in the hot sun. I was tired, so it was time for something different. My language skills were limited to "Hello, how are you?" and "Namaste." So, I resorted to *Jesus, I trust in You* and *Mary, I take refuge in you*. The kids got the first one down pretty well until it became mantra-like. We repeated these phrases a bunch of times. They smiled, yes, the kids were excited to be learning English.

When I returned to my room an hour later, a fellow pilgrim walked in, clearly upset – even his eyes snarled! He said, "Do you realize that the seminarians and priests have to stay here after we leave?" I was baffled and asked him to clarify. Still glaring, he said that Christians were being persecuted in-country for believing in Jesus. My teaching those children Jesus's name put them at risk *and* the Jesuits teaching them! Not sure what I looked like, but no doubt my mouth hung open. Finally, I said that I wasn't aware that I'd put anyone under threat, then thanked him for correcting me.

That I felt acutely embarrassed and dumbfounded would be an understatement. Yes, it hurt, and what was all the more earthshaking – the man's demeanor was so totally different than his usual affable self. A day later, we were friendly again. In life, we might get blindsided. Take the good *and* bad lessons from the situation. Some lessons sting, but don't ignore them.

Deeds not Words. Do acts of love. My dad, who hails from the "old school", often says, "*Show* me, don't tell me…" For me, this can mean something simple, like picking up trash, emptying the dishwasher, sending flowers to a loved one, encouraging a friend, inspiring someone to volunteer at a soup kitchen. Translation in these instances means, after talking, always follow-through with action. My problem? I talk a good game, and actually have good intentions, but sometimes, I fail to follow through. As I've no doubt mentioned before, I remain a work-in-progress. I needed during the pilgrimage not only to preach and inspire folks to service, but also to get in the trench and get my hands dirty (or clean if washing dishes was called for!).

Find your gift and use it. Some are good at planning, others at cooking. Our youth were especially good at keeping a light attitude with jokes and games. Serving on pilgrimage is serious business – leaving sin behind, becoming holy, more or less. At times, things got very tense – negotiating with traffic cops, cab drivers or airline agents, and hoping you didn't offend anyone. Adults carried the burdens, looked suitably grim – in other words we were keeping things on track. Our youth brought us needed refreshment with jokes and light attitudes, even singing songs from a movie or the radio. It helped us older folks greatly, when heavy details were wearing us down, after all, *we* were on pilgrimage to have fun, too!

One of the biggest challenges of our pilgrimage was getting on the right train and keeping our luggage together. Not easy in the huge, bustling station at Sealdah. This was a microcosm of the macro, in this case, like the streets of Calcutta, only scaled-down. There were still tons of people, beggars, entrepreneurs, vendors, wandering tourists, attendants and traffic cops. We found the right entrance portal, while threading our way through taxis, buses and cows. Staying together took a lot of work. We watched for the train, kept an eye on our luggage, avoided opportunistic beggars and entrepreneurs, and still stayed aware of each other. Perhaps the sense of threat heightened our awareness. Hyper-alertness is useful for tourists, after all, we're targets of opportunity. This was true on the streets when we travelled as a group.

The man on a cot–different roles to play. When we were going through the Jesu Ashram Leprosarium, we got a tour by the head-Jesuit priest there. It was a little nerve-racking for most visitors – seeing another leprosarium up close. It was a sprawling place. As we walked through, in the middle of the courtyard was what looked like a man, or at least a body, very skeletal-like. I went out to bless him, and was a little intimidated by his appearance and sickness; he looked like a human corpse. But he slowly opened his eyes and as it happened, I was trying to be very gentle, using a hushed voice and then our Jesuit began speaking very strongly, awakening the man. The sick man slightly moved his eyes. I gave him a blessing. Immediately, I heard singing. Our group was nearby. One of our pilgrims led a song, it was soothing-wafting and sonorous amidst the clamor and misery around us. It spiritually uplifted me and the man, I think, maybe somehow, this assisted his healing.

Another time, we had to definitely work together, utilizing our meager Bengali: We were trying to get train tickets at a rail counter, super-hyped, mobs of people all around, not to mention the stress of talking to Indians we couldn't understand. Eventually, we got through to the ticket-agent, and he got through to us, a miracle in itself. Our Bengali was awful, and hand gestures were equally ineffective.

Whether you're in stressful situations or even if things are benign, you can always use help. Having a good team to help is a blessing, and you will probably learn something new.

When I look back at our India pictures, my favorite ones are the group shots (especially at Kanchenjunga mountain), and (usually) with everyone smiling, saluting and enjoying the moment. The energetic appearances hold a magnetic quality —being part of the Mystical Body of Christ is a joy and we have the records to prove it! Of course, once again, it's proof that a group going through things together is better than a lone individualist trying to overcome mountainous challenges.

CHAPTER 8

*"You cannot be half a saint; you must be
a whole saint or no saint at all."*
-St. Therese of Lisieux

Detachment

When you travel anywhere – particularly to India – you'll see many opportunities to surrender, and abandon all to God. It's one of those Life Lessons. *Physically* you may separate from favorite foods, comfort zones and friends, but *metaphysically,* you might even detach from your everyday pedestrian self and old, worn-out beliefs.

Remember it this way: There is much to learn and experience when we gain in *freedom by detachment.* There is a certain pain that comes with detachment – it will feel like pulling physical Velcro from ourselves – but in the end, the old adage is so true: No pain, no gain. Once we detach, better yet, *as* we detach, we grow, become liberated and spiritually mature. God is opening us up for better things and experiences when we let go of old patterns.

Detachment means release, but oppositely, it also means gaining something, or rather Some*one*, better, because you have been freed to do so. As you travel, learn to free yourself from hometown ways and learn new ones. This includes comfortable cars, taking regular showers, eating familiar food, spending time with friends and family.

India gave us plenty of time to go through a great deal of "freeing pain."

Unfortunately, detachment has a bad name in the modern world, conjuring images of monks hibernating in cold caves, enduring intimidating poverty, while mumbling constant, mind-numbing chants—you get the picture.

A key to the virtue of detachment is adding a word in front of it, think of it as *loving* detachment. It makes a difference, making it a more attractive process – certainly more palatable, and keeps it personal. In this way, detachment is a virtue (with virtue defined as a *holy habit*). This will make us more human, not less. In loving detachment, we still need certain people and possessions, but the virtue – and knowing that detachment *is* a virtue– helps us determine which persons or things are really needed, that we may properly strive for balance somewhere in between the extremes of impoverishment and materialism.

Here's my point: in India you'll confront two fundamental facts: 1) How other people live so simply, often in extreme poverty, and from this, 2) Realize how much you've "over-lived", accumulated stuff and gotten rather attached to *having*.

A pilgrimage is prime time for conversion, and gives you opportunity to assess, then *re*-assess how to live liberated (or detached) from those things you've accumulated. Obviously, this must apply to your life choices during pilgrimage, but more importantly, it must apply after you return home. Somehow, you must keep fresh that pilgrimage-momentum!

While in India, because of extreme heat, unrelenting traffic noise and strange food, I was plagued with sheer fatigue. The Pilgrimage seemed a battle between the self that wanted to keep serving, and body that demanded I conserve personal energy. The result? I never got enough sleep, and had to bump down personal expectations, forcing me to reassess how much I could realistically do. It was hard to admit that sometimes, I *had* to rest or take a nap. It didn't matter what else was going on, my body was out of gas.

Other detachments presented themselves upon arrival—internet access was limited and slow, sodas were in bottles or cans and never cold. The streets weren't ever going to be clean, the bedroom wasn't comfortable, and my favorite junk food did not exist here. Realizing I had to do without was a kind of forced freedom, required me to adjust, so, I got used to the scent of pungent herbs, ate stir-fried everything, drank bottled water, watched Bollywood, dealt with impossible phones, crowded streets and uncontrollable dogs. This was pilgrimage.

And, before you ask, yes, I went through separation anxiety even before leaving home – already stressing, because I knew what wouldn't be obtainable in India. But, you know, after a short time on pilgrimage, I didn't miss that cold soda. What we *think* we need – our allurements and addictions – happen because we've trained ourselves to need them; but through *the process* of loving detachment, we can become new creatures.

The Process:

Awareness -conscious that I am overly-attached and need to be freed;

Breaking the actual chain of addiction -both the desire to have, and the physical reaction of needing;

Connecting to a new way of being – accepting and liking it, the "new normal"- which is better than always "fighting things off".

It won't happen all at once, but will occur with spiritual practice and God's Grace (His divine life within). Only then will we be able to let go of attachments and realize something profound: *What was all the fuss about in the first place?*

Containers. We humans generally use "mental containers" to understand life, situations, people and jobs. We have ready-made receptacles, thoughts or ideas, for most of our experiences. So, in dealing with various temperaments, we create character profiles. Personalities and nationalities each have special labels. But, there's one problem. A thought-container isn't useful if what you jam inside it doesn't fit. On pilgrimage, it's prudent to accept new situations on its own merits – difficult for some American travelers to India because they want to "fix" everything, make it more like what they've already experienced back home. India has too many variations and nothing about the place will never fit into any container. Take my advice. Don't try to "fix" things in India; let them be – better yet, just be in the moment.

Change of focus. When we feel hunger-pangs at home, it's easy to find sustenance – from the pantry, fridge, grocery store or quickie-mart. The concept of going hungry is alien to many in America – with so much fast-food available all over and nearby just about anyone, a foreigner probably thinks all Americans obsess about eating. Certainly we pilgrims in Calcutta went hungry, at least for a while – sometimes for most of a given day. Sure, we knew (hoped) there would be a dinner somewhere, eventually. Most days, dinner wasn't a big spread. We ate sparingly, and got used to it. We had beds with blankets during our time in India, and access to food on a fairly-regular basis. Other people in-country weren't so fortunate. That put things in perspective. Thinking the right way means being grateful for what I did have.

Me, a *missionary*? It was an epiphany, I like doing missionary work and yet never thought of myself as a missionary. How did this happen? Slowly, like a lot of things in life. Drip by drip, the Colorado River carved the Grand Canyon, creating incredible beauty. The same thing can happen to you! You should take a trip overseas, and then another one, your mind and heart *will* expand. Then do some service overseas, and your heart expands even more. Add in personal challenges, curve balls, surprises, hardships, blessings, all these things add up to a pattern of transformation.

The things we left behind us – friends, familiar rituals, prized possessions – and getting into the groove of India – that was my heart expanding for me. I learned surrender and detachment, stopped clinging to what was missing, appreciated anew what was around me, found joy in service, beauty in doing humble things, and found something profound had happened – I had grown spiritually. At least a little.

Returning. I was kind of sad coming back home to the States. Why?

1-I was returning to my same old routine. I had developed a taste for the exotically- different.

2-I missed my new friends, and the intimate community of my fellow pilgrims to India. We'd had two weeks of prayer, work, fun, and challenges. As a result, we became closer and more reliant upon one another.

3-Imissed India itself, with all of the excitement and thrill of adventure, the smells, the colors, the people, the frenetic pace of life, in spite of my occasional complaints and personal squabbles.

4-I missed being *away* – happily disconnected from my personal and public life, and out of the rat race.

As St. Augustine prayed, "Our hearts are restless…" While being away is refreshing, renewing and necessary in some ways, we must remember not to romanticize being away, and long for another adventure as an only means of salvation. We need to deal with what's in front of us and just *be* in the present moment – whether it's boring or exciting. In the long term, it's best not to rely on escapes and exit strategies to fulfill us. Yes, pilgrimages can help us get with the bigger picture of life, and can help us make decisions regarding the smaller pictures– change them around, re-prioritize them now and again. In essence, we should go from routine to a new rhythm.

While I was kind of down once returning home, I also knew from other pilgrimages I've taken – seeds of truth and inspiration and love had been implanted in me. Those seeds would bear fruit at a later time. I wasn't worried that any lesson would go to waste, or that I would squander God's generosity and His many blessings. I know pilgrimages are a graced time, during and afterwards, when you can find and learn more deeply about God showing Himself to us, *and* how He wants us to grow, learn and live.

Don Piper, author of *90 Minutes in Heaven*, spoke of a "the new normal – finding that new groove after a pivotal event becomes a new way of being..." I knew I'd have to consciously work at that once back home. I had a profound, pivotal experience seeing India's poverty – it had affected me deeply, so: How to share my inner growth with others was a big job in the offing.

Being a seasoned traveler has its perks – people who have never done it ask advice from me. A parishioner was planning a trip to Mexico, and asked for prayers. Why? The trip was a week away, and she hadn't yet received her passport. She needed me to storm heaven and I did, her passport arrived three days later. Then she asked for more prayers, the lady was a nervous traveler. She wants to go away, but started missing home even before she left: *Who'll feed the dog?...The world can't go on without me.* To summarize, being out of her routine made the woman overly-anxious; she wasn't equipped to deal with unknowns, when the other shoe would drop. In essence, being in the moment wasn't a lesson she had learned deeply enough.

Let's just say I could have given her a ton of advice, but she would have collapsed from the sheer volume of my data dump. Some people learn better by doing—and simple words as its hard to cut through the density and opaqueness of anxiety.

Insight –I once read an article on storage-space warehousing, highlighting the rise of this unique American phenomenon. Have you noticed? In the west and India, we were surrounded by excess – in the west, it's the accumulation of *things,* too much – we're suffocating from the sheer volume of it. On the other hand, in India, excess is its extreme poverty.

Do we need all the things we have? Do we even want them all? Yet, stuff still seems to collect in our homes, we keep holding on to things—and junk, for whatever reason. Some are shopaholics and can't resist a "deal". Other people could care less – both extreme views.

As with a lot of things, we need balance and the virtue-practice of renunciation – to not give in to collecting or buying stuff. Sometimes circumstances dictate what you keep and what you give away. Once, I was moving to a new posting and went through my book collection, *Did I need them all?* No. I grabbed about seven books to give away, out of a hundred. A week later, I went through the shelves again, and still again. I once thought these particular books were like gold, but they no longer held any power over me. It was easy to let go of a dozen of them, and still more. Some things we need and many we obviously don't.

In India we needed *some* things – an international phone, water, Gatorade; food; medical supplies; clothes, personal items, basics – but not too much else, including sleep and resting periods.

Elegant simplicity. That's what we saw in the Missionaries of Charity, in other Catholic orders, Buddhist monks, Hindu savants, Amish families, among the homeless. It's a kind of primordial and visceral truth. Use what you need, as little as possible, and do it with grace.

CHAPTER 9

"Do not be afraid. Open wide the doors to Christ."
-Pope St. John Paul II

Universality

UNIVERSALISM

This clunky term means many things. In Calcutta, it means masses of different people and events converging in a way you'll never see anywhere else – it's the ultimate melting-pot. Some places on Earth are polar opposites of Calcutta, small, intimate, and familiar, where nothing much changes – such as where I live in Hancock. Most of my neighbors are locals who grew up there and choose to stay. I find it fun, healing and therapeutic, as I can hear birds, and go for a walk near a peaceful river– and most certainly, I am not racing around with my hair on fire!

Even if you've been in a large city, Calcutta is in a class by itself. The best word to describe it: *Cosmopolitan.* To use a colloquial term, it's a hodge-podge: rich and dirt-poor, shopkeepers and stree kids, tradesmen and technicians, vendors and gnarly entrepreneurs; a gigantic stream of people from all over India converge on Calcutta. As in America, where people are seldom alike, not all Indians are the same color, or religion, clothing is wildly contrasting, depending on traditions, and doesn't seem to vary, regardless what month it is, and everyone moves at top speed.

Calcutta will present you with challenges to your ability to endure, but push through, and find a reason to enjoy it. That goes for any place you'll end up while travelling: Wherever you are, enjoy it, soak up its uniqueness – instead of pining for wherever "the grass is greener:, being always dissatisfied. St. Paul says in Philippians: "For I have learned, in whatever situation I find myself, to be self-sufficient" (4:11). Hmmm, curious, seeing how much Paul traveled after conversion, then he was put under house arrest. He was able to adapt to new ways of living – and so can we!

So, the best general advice I can give myself (yes, I need constant reminders) and others: Look on where you are, and totally *be* in each place, as if it's the best location in which you could ever live – look on it as a once-in-a-lifetime opportunity, because it really is.

As a slight digression, pilgrimaging means not only "going through" a land but also *undergoing* it and sincerely embracing its peoples and ways. Oppositely, tourism is merely visiting a place, viewing people, taking pictures for looking at later, images without heart or soul. Viewing pictures from a pilgrimage is totally different, you feel the spiritual tug and regeneration of the heart, as you recall each encounter – to include joys and sorrows of the people you'd met. Those people spoke to you and gave you their lessons as you gave yourself to them – enabling you to live more thankfully. My soul's microchip is filled to the brim with color, emotion, flavors, incredible diversity, an entire tapestry, but almost no actual photographs. Thanks to digital photography, the pain of developing film has been eliminated, I could take pictures anywhere, if needed. However, I stopped taking photos long ago, as the point of pilgrimaging is giving and enjoying. It's not a documentary pic-taking process!

Why do I like traveling? I want to experience new things, people and places. This is, mind you, a paradox for many people. Most of us are creatures of habit, and we like simple, expected, unchanging routines. Those who won't travel have no interest in changing anything they do. But for ones like me who have been bitten by the "travel bug," we seek the different and exotic. India has all that, and more.

How exotic? Try tasting curry at just about every culinary encounter —even for breakfast! For city-dwellers, seeing lines of taxis isn't unusual – in Calcutta, try thousands of them, and hundreds of motor scooters, plus their stinky exhausts at all hours. Water buffalo might be wandering the streets; people will be bathing in full view; beggars of all descriptions will come at you continuously. As a first-time visitor to Calcutta, all this will be beyond overwhelming.

Your choice. Prepare to embrace it or don't bother traveling to India. You'd be missing marvelous moments, however – like playing with kids on the street in the spray of a hydrant. The physical challenges make it difficult to mentally block out the pollution, a constant, nagging cough, but as you *are* on pilgrimage, and have hopefully been warned on what to expect… go with the flow.

What I have been trying to impart to you, Dear Reader? India is incredibly different – more different than could be imagined, which is part of its allure. There is nothing like it in the ubiquitous strip-mall back home. First-time exposure to Asian culture is mind-boggling, and for the most part, has little-or-nothing connectable to American expectations. Many places have no electricity, or it's unreliable. Most certainly, the food is different, and no one speaks English – that's a given. Unless you have already been exposed to Indian food, or live in a city with pockets of diversity, like I said somewhere else in this book, "Toto, we're not in Kansas anymore!" Stand by for extremely-different everything! No burgers or fries? Fine! Bring on that curried-chicken and eggs masala!

You have an opportunity. Go from being a student of other cultures to becoming a pilgrim, and so embrace diversity by living in it. Let these experiences improve your ability to adapt, enabling your openness to change. Life on the move means breaking out of our comfort zones; otherwise, how boring if nothing ever changed.

We pilgrims experienced different sides of God's revelation while travelling – kind of like viewing a diamond in its many facets. When we truly encountered and immersed ourselves within Calcutta's culture, we experienced the genuine different-ness of God's people, and met various souls of the caste-system, Hindus, Buddhists, spiritual seekers of enlightenment, Catholic religious sisters, temple priests, flight attendants, bell hops, security personnel, street vendors, homeless ones, beggars, shop owners, so many more.

Just so you know, India is a subcontinent, not just a country – it encompasses lush tropical gardens in the south (Goa and Madras) and the coasts, east and west (Chennai/Madras); the plains of middle desert (Agra, location of the Taj Mahal) and the Himalayas in the north, along with Kashmir; and don't forget perpetually-humid Calcutta and Mumbai (Bombay).

WHO YOU'LL MEET ALONG THE WAY!

In Darjeeling, as if the sight of the majestic Kanchenjunga mountain wasn't dramatic enough, while gazing at that heavenly mountain, along comes a brightly-dressed group of ladies in bold outfits, with much fanfare. Turned out they were a native dance troupe from east India. Here's the irony: *They* wanted to take pictures with *us*! They were such a delight, and seemed as fascinated with us as we were with them. In this way, we made new friends. This was a special blessing of God that let us stretch our boundaries and enjoy His infinitude!

I could go on and on with who we met in Calcutta, from the most unusual of places: Two young ladies from Chile – like us, they came to serve at Prem Dan, vagabonds, old-and-young hippies, Australians, Dutch, Germans, Italians and French, many liked to congregate on Sutter Street – a shopping venue with cafes and western-style places, like a mini-San Francisco.

One thing I tried subtly to teach our pilgrims (and learn myself!) was not to be judgmental. If there's any place in the world this could happen, it is in India, with so much poverty, the caste system, its treatment of women. They do things a different way. Is it better or worse? We should respect legitimate differences, learn from them and suspend judgment. Obviously, there are differences in various cultures and even some glaring injustices – remember Gandhi's experiment against the caste system? It didn't always go well. So, that said, it is tricky business to judge different-ness.

Since familiar western-style foods weren't to be found, yearning for them made no sense. Some pilgrims were experimental and adventurous with Indian cuisine, while others were prudent and conservative. One good thing, Indians –and most of the world in general – don't eat big meals, like many Americans expect, in other words, there are no super-size portions. We learned to operate on smaller meals.

One of the joyful aspects of Calcutta is meeting Missionaries of Charity sisters from all over the world. Of course, most are from India and as noted earlier, MC houses are practically global – but some are from Africa (The Congo, Kenya, Nigeria), South America, Europe. If you meet one, you meet them all. That's a compliment. They all have a similar spirit – love of God, love of their religion, love for serving the poor, they possess a great cheer about it all.

INCULTURATION

On the Ganges river on an extremely hot day

While we talk a good game about immersing ourselves in other peoples' culture, we sometimes fail to do it, but others *do*. The buzz-word within contemporary Christianity and missions these days is *inculturation*. Translated: As a Christian missionary, one must grow into the culture, learn from it, and respect it long before even thinking of converting anyone, if ever. Forget the days when nuns and priests went directly into jungles and foreign villages and threw crucifixes around, seemingly "laying down the law of love". Back then, the mandate was to *convert*; missionaries encouraged natives to become baptized, or asked first and fed folks later. I realize that's a rough caricature of the past, but unfortunately, sometimes it happened that way. Today, a more balanced view would be to win the hearts of the locals and then *suggest* conversion, maybe.

Sometimes today, conversion (the word itself is suspect) is not even mentioned, or isn't an issue in religious circles, particularly Catholics. Simply put, charity, justice, agriculture projects and handing out food have become main purposes of Faith. Somewhere between the extremes of laxity and naïveté is the "perfect middle" where respect goes with religion and charity, with Christ's saving grace. Invitation is given in place of imposition. As usual, we need both inculturation and incarnation.

Now, follow *this* story of inculturation. There was once a European lady who became a nun and then traveled to Ireland to become "someone else" – someone more Catholic and Christian, in religious life as a sister. What she already did wasn't enough. Then she was sent to India to go further, and more deeply into the Christ. She had been reading the Gospels – which are about a Jewish preacher – adopted impoverished habits and aligned herself with the rejected and poor, and continually spoke of a Kingdom that is accessible by everyone – especially the un-elite. That's inculturation. Of course, we are talking about Mother Teresa.

Before she ever began the Missionaries of Charity, Mother Teresa donned the sari of Indian ladies rather than the religious garb of westerners. While minimizing her English, she learned and mastered a Bengali dialect. She befriended lepers and empowered the middle class to help the poor. She ate like a typical Indian poor person – with fingers, not utensils. She even begged. She was conservative in some ways (conserving energy and loving sacred tradition), liberal in others. She gave away tons of food, clothes, time, love, in short, her whole life to God and others. She became inculturated precisely by un-becoming her old self.

Somehow, in all this, Mother Teresa was treated like a rock star, sometimes with glitz and also with praise and the utmost respect. Part of the mystique of Calcutta is because of the Missionaries of Charity and the "spiritual wake" created by Mother Teresa – whether intended or not. Herein is a real lesson of universalism-inculturation!

A group of 30 of us once went to a large Missionary of Charity house in Washington, D.C., and saw a "mini-universe" of people – black and white, Hispanic and European, poor folks who'd been there a while, and others just newly-arrived. We brought a diverse group of young and old pilgrims with us and served those in the house – living in the sprawling grounds. Some had AIDs and tuberculosis, some were street people and others were just down on their luck. It was what I had come to expect, as I have seen MC facilities all over the world.

Our volunteers that day cleaned the chapel (which was pretty clean to begin with – MCs are fastidious), some worked on flower beds (reminiscent of India), while others visited various patients and clients. Later we served the men and women their evening meal, and celebrated Mass. Some of the clients joined us in the chapel – the high point of our visit.

What did we learn? Many of our volunteers had never met any MC sisters and were impressed by their joy and spirit of service – especially the ones from India. They also learned about service – many clients were poor, and this encounter proved a learning opportunity on how to talk to people, how to treat them with dignity – attempting to see Christ in each person – one of the main messages of Mother Teresa. This unique encounter took us into another world – the world of poor, broken people, and while many didn't know how to carry on a conversation with such different folks, we stressed what was more important. Just be with them, no talking, no *doing*, just visiting with them in a communion of love. This was a hard concept for some of us, as many want to solve things and produce results.

We have to re-calibrate ourselves in life to embrace new ways of being and forge a different track of life when dealing with others. While we may be awkward at first, the process will become easier. It's a new way of being – doing things in ways we could not foresee.

Befriend. One thing you learn on pilgrimage is to become friendly, or you will wilt, well, almost. We all need friendship, companionship – humans are social beings. And this is especially true if travelling outside your culture without command of the local language. Whether travelling with a group or alone, you (gradually) learn to make friends – at least most people do. There are, of course, those rare souls who like being alone 24/7. Not many of those, Peter, my British friend in Darjeeling comes to mind.

Small Becomes Large. Travelling to India is a shot in the gut about poverty, the meaning of life and this question: *Where is God in all this?* You witness garbage dumps where children pick through them for food, see beggars on the streets, endure the public bathrooms and washrooms. It would be hard to start pitying oneself after this. It's a mindset, getting out of your province, state, district, and your own head, finally seeing the Big Picture. It's those Big Stories which inspire and, frankly, can embarrass us– like Francis Xavier sailing across the world; Joseph Benedict Labre walked across Europe and lived homeless, pretty intense stuff. Hopefully, your conscience will convict you!

A world map in the Motherhouse showed all the places the Missionaries of Charity sisters were serving. They truly are universal. Most were in India, but there was a fairly even distribution of dots through the whole world, demonstrating just how widespread MCs are.

Seeing (and feeling) the Big Picture must have affected a lot of people, since volunteers showed up in Calcutta from everywhere. I had something in common with everyone in that MC house – all of us wanted to serve and honor the Lord in the poor.

S.O.S. It's not what you think! It is defined thus: *Strategies of Surrender*. Such as when we consciously put ourselves in harm's way. Example: When a fellow pilgrim took care of a diseased patient at Kalighat, making himself vulnerable to that disease. We might undergo affliction and give up creature comforts, such as giving away your meal to someone poor, and much hungrier than you. When we do this, we voluntarily enter into the mysterious, and that which is veiled –first learning to crawl, then to walk, and becoming truly mature.

Surrender is not always easy for some westerners. Realities like assimilation, enculturation and transformation are not naturally second-nature. It's not all about conquering something, but daring to go into foreign places, unable to read a single sign, visiting and serving in AIDS homes, exposing yourself to airborne sicknesses, and surprising yourself when you get used to it, and bend with the adventure.

The mystical body of Christ –many parts of Christian members, one Lord – will help the disciple do the growing needed, and at a rapid pace. James Joyce famously said, "The Catholic church— here comes everyone." Point is, you aren't joining a bunch of ranting robots, but a group of diverse, interesting human beings, not necessarily a like-minded organization, but one in which you can grow.

DIVERSITY=INDIA

Poverty. It's in your face and unrelenting. Realize you can become part of it or be an observer.

Transportation. Railroads, trains and buses, taxis are available, even rickshaws.

Drinks. The tea is great, and *lati* – a creamy, cool fruit drink, along with sugary coffee and the occasional Indian cola.

Races / Classes. There are hundreds of tribes, and myriad races all over India. And although most westerners can't distinguish one from the other, the Indians can. They are very class-conscious, aware of their social standards and want to be counted as individuals.

Just so you know, there are many rich people in India; the global economy will probably make more. They live in nice houses on nice streets, but a block over, you'll see kids in a trash heap looking for food.

Weather. It's a big factor for India, at times, and depends on what part of the subcontinent you're going, that tells you what clothes to pack. As described throughout this book, Calcutta is hot and humid at all times of the year – there is no cool season.

Cleanliness. There are different levels of hygiene in India, and again, it depends on where you are. The Missionaries of Charity houses are clean, health-inspector-ready, but the same cannot be said for the poor the MCs serve. **Contrast:** The Oberoi hotel was immaculate, but on the sidewalks just outside, it's chaotic and filthy. Streets are usually passable, sometimes modern-looking, but not generally clean. Dust is everywhere, inside and out, so don't expect clean air, especially in Calcutta.

One thing. Once the local population finds out you're from the U.S., well, they expect certain things from you, sometimes money, goodwill, or a connection. They sometimes think we walk on streets of gold and we're all millionaires, it depends on the political climate. Locals also believe most Americans who visit India are do-gooders and can sometimes perform miracles… and they think Americans smile all the time! Wow.

CHAPTER 10

"Let us go forward in peace, our eyes upon
heaven, the only one goal of our labors."
-St. Therese of Lisieux

Conclusions

I received a call a couple years back, that sounded something like this: "Hey-ho, it's freezing now. Do you remember when we were in cold Darjeeling, trying to keep warm? Give me a call back…"

It seems I'm so far away from India, but then, I hear that phone message, and suddenly I'm instantly there. Some part of me *wants* to be there, and it's as if I can taste it all again.

One might call it an inspirational spark – when only a few words move you into a zone of instant remembrance, with all the delight, feelings and thoughts intact.

When I scan pictures of India, see an Indian movie, or talk to a fellow pilgrim about a past journey, somehow, I totally overlook the stress experienced while traveling so far away, and mentally bypass the hassles experienced when there, I accentuate the sweet spots and good times.

For better or worse, in such instances, I become Pollyanna-like, seeing and remembering only good things. Removed are those challenges of packing, waiting, trying to interpret languages, getting the right money, dealing with strange food, and all the rest, handling a pilgrim's problems, etc. Our young people no doubt remember it fondly, only because they never dealt with the planning process. Being spontaneous worked for them, and they totally enjoyed seeing new places, meeting new people, and simply focusing on adventure and joy of the moment. I'm thinking the young ones' outlook, that ability to grab onto joy, would help us "older folk" enjoy travel much more!

Inspiration. Near Mardighara during our 2005 pilgrimage, we visited a Jesuit house of young men who were becoming fully-professed Jesuits – this was just after we'd toured the leprosarium and were quite exhilarated, even if a bit tired. We entered a classroom of 25 young seminarians. They smiled as we walked in – and stood respectfully to greet us. After an awkward moment, I introduced our group, said who we were and spontaneously launched into my biography, and encouraged these young men in their pursuit of the priesthood and a religious life. Then I asked each of our visitors – six others – to introduce themselves and they did – totally alight with new fire at this encounter, and encouraged by those young seminarians' infectious zeal.

I then asked the Jesuit headmaster-instructor if the young men could introduce themselves. They each said their name and a little about themselves, and why they wanted to be a Jesuit and a priest. Yes, they were shy, but zealous, and to summarize, they said simply and quite innocently that they wanted to serve Jesus and His people.

I was so impressed by their sincerity – that they truly wanted to carry Jesus's message of salvation to others. Simple and yet so refreshing. Without intellectualism or technical language, these young men cut through it all and offered a fresh approach to vocation and discipleship! I learned once again of simplicity, and of these young men's thirst for Our Lord, focusing on the Message.

Later, we toured their quarters – a room about 30-by-15 feet, and yes, twenty of them lived in that room! Each had a single-sized rack for a bed. Some stored their few possessions on one end of the rack. That was it. These young men were surely sacrificing!

WHAT DO I MISS ABOUT INDIA?

- Dodging traffic as soon as I'd step onto the sidewalk – plus the energy and excitement.
- Closeness that grew from traveling with fellow pilgrims. One of the biggest transitions for me, a celibate priest, was coming back, waking up in an empty room, and realizing I had a whole day to myself. No pilgrimage schedule of prayer, service, dinner and touring.
- Children in Calcutta streets, as they smiled and played with us.
- Seeing bright-colored saris, their lovely drapery and tasteful elegance.
- Seeing how many people could cram into an Indian taxi, or how many more could fit into an already overcrowded bus!
- Men getting haircuts on the street.
- Pilgrims doing laundry and seeing soap suds float down the alleyways.
- The rugged hills of Darjeeling.
- Bright colors of the markets, the smells of street cafes, seeing open fires on the streets.
- Cheerful MC sisters working hard, and smiling so much, that they radiated gladness.

My friend, Father Jim Farmer, recently underwent an operation, and quoted a friend, who had died in the last year. "Count your blessings more than your pains..." There's an immediacy of truth to that. We all have pains in life and need to focus on joys and blessings instead, lest the difficulties overwhelm us and we fixate too much on pain.

Reminders. Indian restaurants are not a dime a dozen in the U.S. – especially where I live. But when I came upon one in Hagerstown, it evoked instant reminders of India and suddenly, I've got to have curried vegetables and hot lentil soup! While dining in this place with a friend, we talked to the manager, who really was from India, and asked, "What brought you to the States, and to Hagerstown, of all places?" His answer: "Destiny." It made me laugh, as that I'd heard that word in *Slumdog Millionaire*. Yes, Destiny made sure two lovers met, and that the hero would win a million bucks. That's what it means, in part, to be Indian or Hindu, understanding that Destiny has a hand in your life, we Christians should understand that concept as well. Destiny has another label – God's Providence.

Change. When you go on a pilgrimage, you come back looking virtually the same, hopefully, however, you will be different inside. Because of encounters with strangers, the service work you did, the new foods you ate, the pilgrim-friends you made, the fantastic places toured, you couldn't help but change inside. The question is, as with all pilgrimages: how much did you change? And, for how long did this change continue, how deeply did it go? Obviously, a pilgrimage won't do this overnight. Many pilgrims who go want to change, but find that difficult (what else is new?). Yet, the seeds have been planted inside, and like all seeds, they have to germinate. Growth is latent, and waiting within. It is up to each pilgrim who has made pilgrimage to India to amalgamate their varied experiences, let those seeds grow and begin the process of *continual* change.

Contrast the "bigness" of an Indian pilgrimage with the quaintness of coming home, and going back to the same pattern: Taking out the trash, being patient with parents, dealing with a difficult person… it's mundane, after being on such an exotic adventure. Your friends and colleagues might have expected an "enlightened" outlook from you, that's not always the case. I struggle with this expectation every time I when return from pilgrimage, and think: *Can I really translate the pilgrimage thrills and deep lessons into my present, daily, hum-drum world?* And the answer? I'm still working on it!

As we have noted many times, there was considerable drama while working with the Missionaries of Charity – they literally rescued people, especially children. It inspired me, because at some level, I wanted to become like them, and become a change-agent in the world.

Hopefully, change is possible, that within, one can transform into someone new. Maybe there would be a *new* adage. You *can* teach an old dog new tricks. Admittedly, change takes perseverance.

Do *you* want to change? Become someone else? If you don't have an inner fire moving you into becoming that "someone else", change can't happen. Generating desire needs an outside catalyst, like going on pilgrimage, volunteering service, finding a need to help others and being able to fill that need. Until then, change cannot take place. Remember this formula:

Desire + Follow-through + Discipline = Change. It takes all these elements.

Many people (like myself) find it difficult to make changes, because when you start, two things likely happen: When the going gets tough, you go back to the familiar and comfortable (old habits, routines and behaviors), or you give up altogether, because you don't have the gumption, lack desire, or simply don't want to navigate among landmines littering your personal landscape.

Change is hard. Cardinal Newman once said, "To live is to change, and to be perfect is to have changed much." So, I'm thinking, that after these Indian pilgrimages: I went to India, experienced awesome and awe-inspiring drama, and came back to my same old life. Now, I'm depressed because after tasting all that different-ness, I thought change was possible, and yet here it is, months and years later – I'm the same person inside. Did I 'miss the boat' of conversion? The answer is, *No, you haven't. Keep going, and keep the conversion flowing.*

The seeds are there. Fertilize them!

SURPRISES and SAME OLD…

You go away on pilgrimage looking for *someone or something Big*, like Mother Teresa, the thrill of enlightenment, changing yourself, and yet, you might not get what you want, but may find unexpected epiphanies instead. Welcome them!

Contrariwise, you'll find the world over that human nature is, human nature. As they say today, "It is what it is." In Indian airports and train stations, entrepreneurs tried their best to get our attention and make money off us. Some were aggressive, some respectful and others demanding. Other times, we met people on the street while walking to our service place and asked for directions, they tried and were sincere —these were "little helps" along the Way of the Pilgrimage.

If you treat people nicely, they'll treat you back the same. That's true everywhere. People don't change because human nature doesn't change.

Beyond Within
White saris amidst clamoring chaos,
Charity passing in the streets:
Eternity etches the mind.

That is how I see the Missionaries of Charity amidst Calcutta chaos.

Another reason people travel to India – to witness something *super*natural, not just the market place, pipe-and-cobra dens, plush Persian rugs, the crowds and the ashrams. Everyone knows about and desires the *super*natural – that is, SOMEONE who is different, not part of the mundane here-and-now – something really, out of this world. The sense of supernatural-ness is encoded in our DNA and inhabits our deep desires.

We are made from something else, created from *Some*one else and FOR this Someone Else. This super-nature, trans-natural, Un-created, is what we are looking for in each and every encounter of life, in each new experience, in every daily-boring-bland breakthrough encounter. Not only that. It is *within* us —impelling us to seek different-ness, things above-it-all. People look in odd places for it – sports, hobbies, sex, intellectual pursuits, or within religion.

The supernatural is not divorced from this world, not completely above or beyond it, it is awaiting discovery of its alleged aloofness. Maybe that's why I am so attracted to India. It's so different and yet so similar and much older than my country. The oldness resides in the burning ghats of Varanasi, Hindu shrines on every Calcutta street corner, incense wafting from a temple, a driver's miniature shrine in his cab, the Muslim call to prayer, Brahmin priests, wandering savants, monks begging, or Missionaries of Charity sisters in action…

In Europe, this supernatural once existed as observed through the great gothic cathedrals which are largely monuments to the past. They stand for what has gone before, speak of the supernatural, for sure – very tangibly, but stand for something or maybe Someone who is *not* there?

The Missionaries of Charity nuns stand out amidst the grime and slime of Calcutta – they are different and at the same time human and accessible. Or put another way, they are the "foreign-as-familiar". We want to see and experience different, supernatural things within our daily world so we, on one hand, don't get bored, and on the other, have some aliveness and different-ness. We all want different-ness in a certain kind of way that's not *too* different!

Some might notice while abroad a striking fatalism, which reigns in the East. There are forces of nature interacting with humans, which religions such as Taoism, Shintoism and Hinduism express, and is found in some Shakespearean tragicomedies. It's all about the individual and his-or-her journey through the world. Basically, this implies humans are merely puppets on a stage, a situation not to our liking, but we have no real, effective choice in the matter.

We have few options (this implies free will!).At one extreme is fatalism, at the other end is unbounded freedom. Somewhere in the middle, drawing from both extremes, is what we shall describe as Christian free will, meaning this equation:

Man + the world's factors + God = human freedom and life in the world.

Indians tend to be more fatalist than westerners. When Mother Teresa started picking up those starving, ragged bodies on the Calcutta streets, she was more-or-less breaking an "Indian law", or put another way: *Don't fool with other people's fate.* And yet, think of the caste system, and inbred poverty, which systemically imprisons individuals to their so-called "station in life." But we Catholics and Christians can lapse, lunge or morph into various positions of the fatalism-freedom continuum, and simply walk by starving people, or fail to help a family member, because "that's life" or "It is what it is" or "It's all good" (even when it obviously isn't). We learned in Calcutta that the MC sisters continually choose to help others and empower their human freedom, even though the odds (or fatalism) are stacked against them.

So, how about you? Where are you in all this?

We're All Pilgrims. So, who goes to India, if it's so different? All kinds of people. From youth and elderly, intellectuals and simpletons, rich and poor, snobs and free spirits – you'll find them all there. "Average people" visit India, too. I met single ladies travelling by themselves, married couples, New-Agers, social activists, conservative Christians, evangelicals, devotees of gurus and so many others.

Now, why do some go? Some go for ayurvedic medicine and treatments, others for enlightenment. Still others seek an escape from the West, and some serve at Kalighat. So even as you might seek diversity and universalism in a far-off land, you gradually learn that people you meet during your travels already have that diversity. Some travel with hardly any luggage, some eat simply (and very cheaply, certainly not in restaurants!).

On the way to India, we met Muslim imams, Catholic priests, Indian families, French tourists and Middle Eastern Arabs. While there, we worked in slums, went to rich houses, to orphanages and celebrated with religious nuns and simple Indian folk.

You have a choice: Stay where you are and the way you are, *or* join the human parade of life. Travel and become a new person by meeting (or bumping into), others a hemisphere away. Expand your horizons and learn about life, or even Eternal Life. The other choice? Stay on Main Street in your hometowns. As Catholics and Christians, we are all pilgrims on the road to Eternal Life – *through* this world. Becoming a global pilgrim will certainly jump-start that process.

One thing is certain. You can't be a nervous sort and travel to India, you have to be adventurous, and unafraid of the new and different. Be an observer or an adventurer…In either case, CHOOSE LIFE!

Namaste!

Dal Lake, Kashmir, in the north, manifests the glories of India!

Lightning Source UK Ltd.
Milton Keynes UK
UKHW040624041222
413302UK00012B/441/J